Other titles from Dr. Nathaniel Stampley, Sr.

Parables of The Kingdom

Introduction to Homiletics

Biblical Commentary on Wisdom Literature

SPIRITSCRIBE PUBLISHING, LLC
P.O. BOX 2241
HUMBLE, TEXAS 77347
www.spiritscribepublishing.com
(832) 445-6229

First Printing: January 2009
Second Printing: June 2009
Third Printing: October 2009
Fourth Printing: March 2011
Fifth Printing: October 2012
Sixth Printing: July 2015
Seventh Printing: January 2017

Understanding Spiritual Gifts and Calling to Ministry

By Nathaniel J. Stampley, Sr.

Printed in the United States of America

ISBN 978-0-615-25460-9

Published by
Stampley Ministries, Inc.
1036 W. Atkinson Avenue
Milwaukee, Wisconsin 53206
Phone: (414) 949-7568
Website: stampleyministries.org
Email: stampleyministries@gmail.com

Acknowledgments

I would be remiss if I did not pause to recognize several individuals who have influenced my life immensely along the way and serve as a constant reminder of what it means to display faithfulness and excellence. My parents, Pastor James and Luetilda Stampley were trailblazers in the Church of God in Christ in the state of Louisiana. They exemplified a life of holiness and instilled in my thirteen siblings and me a sense of belonging to God, family and the community. In addition, they profoundly taught us the value of faith, prayer, compassion, and patience.

Dr. Arenia C. Mallory was a distinguished educator and champion for the underprivileged children in Mississippi at the height of segregation during the last century. She taught us to *"Walk in dignity. Talk in dignity. Live in dignity."* Aside from my parents, she was the most influential person to help shape my character during my formative teen and young adult life.

Dr. Howard Thurman's calling and character distinguished him as a mystic, philosopher, educator, theologian, and pastor.
He was keenly aware of the *Spirit of Truth* and refused to be restricted by labels and traditions.

Dr. James Powell clearly understands what it means to be a pastor, educator, husband, father, and missionary. His passion for helping the disinherited, both domestically and internationally, is remarkable. We share a common vision and that is why since 1969, he has truly been my best friend.

Valerie Davis has been my friend for over 40 years. She willingly accepted the task of editing and proofreading this manuscript. She has graciously accepted this task of managing all aspects of this project. Without her sacrifice I would not have been able to submit this publication in a timely manner. In addition, my dear friends Pat McCoy and Richmond Izard have provided valuable service in reviewing the manuscript. Thank each of you for your labor of love.

Lastly, I want to salute my lovely wife, Carolyn, a retired educator since 1972. Her patience and sense of purpose is simply amazing. I have watched her bring balance, grace and beauty to our marriage, as well as our congregation where she servess alongside me in Pastoral Ministry and Music Ministry. In addition, she served as a teacher in the Milwaukee Public School System. Her talent and passion for the fine arts is being manifested and passed down through our children's performances on Broadway and other venues across America. I admire her tenacity and resolute spirit even when I know she is facing awkward moments. I cannot imagine my life without the gift that God has given me—this adorable saint, Carolyn. In such light, we can all see that gifts and callings are designed to be lived and experienced and not viewed as novelty on the shelf.

Table of Contents

Introduction

For some time, I pondered over the best way to present these lessons. Then, one day while sitting in a Sunday School class, the following verse from the Epistle of James stood out as the basis and inspiration for what I am about to share. *"Every good endowment and every perfect gift is from above, coming down from the Father of lights with whom there is no variation or shadow due to change."* (James 1:17) In other words, we must acknowledge the Most High God as the source and distributor of everything that has eternal value and noteworthy recognition in this world.

Though the spirit of disobedience and rebellion is ever-present on earth to disrupt a harmonious relationship with God and each other, God is the ultimate source of spiritual gifts and callings. Romans 11:29 clearly illustrates that God disbursed gifts and callings in a very serious and permanent manner: *"For the gifts and the call of God are irrevocable."*

Since childhood, I have always inferred from the above scripture that some talented and gifted people don't necessarily adhere to holy lifestyles, but instead use their gifts for Satan. Nowadays I also recognize a deeper revelation in an alternate interpretation of the verse.

For example, the calling of Abraham and the election of the children of Israel in the Old Testament are both mysterious and revealing. As we examine the Abrahamic blessing, we are compelled to wonder what this nation did to merit grace, mercy and favor above all other people. Perhaps Israel's role as nomad or underdog in the midst of other well established nations captured God's attention and compelled Him to catapult the Israelites into becoming "a people unto himself." (Deut 7:6; 14:2; 29:13) Nonetheless this divine intervention by *Yahweh* served as a watershed in Biblical History and at the same time established an everlasting covenant and irrevocable gift that cannot be repealed. In these ways, Yahweh's relationship with Israel, and Christ's relationship with the church, is phenomenal and perpetual.

This great mystery is both based in and revealed through God's holy nature, which can be characterized by righteousness, trustworthiness and faithfulness. Because God is always trustworthy, He promises never to reverse the *heavenly places* embedded in *earthen vessels*. Because God always operates in righteousness, He cannot repent or change His mind. Because God is faithful, He upholds his promise despite the covenant community's periodic and conscious rebelliousness and disobedience.

Therefore, when we observe the community of faith empowered and displaying faithfulness toward their spiritual gifts or callings to

6

ministry we are actually seeing a glimpse of wholesome living, which reflects God's holiness.

While we have already established that the nature of God is holy, let us also recognize that the motivational principle of God is love—a quality that is always exemplified in sacrifice and action.

Since childhood I have always been fascinated with gifted and talented individuals. At the same time, I sensed that my spiritual gifts and a divine calling were waiting for me to discover and embrace them. For me this spiritual awakening and personal journey began in June of 1967, when I accepted my call to ministry. However, it was only after considerable rebellion, apprehension, ignorance, and an array of positive and negative experiences that I became convinced and convicted that I truly had a spiritual mandate to fulfill within the Kingdom of God.

Everyday, I see individuals struggling, rebelling and ignoring their gifts and callings due to a lack of knowledge or spiritual awareness. I am convinced that everyone has a gift or calling that is waiting to be discovered. Because these gifts and calling are designed to make a qualitative difference in the environment in which God has strategically assigned us to work and serve, each of us has to become significantly more alert and responsive.

Therefore, I am inspired to share these revealing lessons surrounding the spiritual and social aspects of life in order to enlighten novice and mature believers, laity and clergy alike. I firmly believe that through proper teaching and increased responsiveness to the calling and needs of ministry, some of us will discover that God has endowed us with multiple gifts.

No one can monopolize spiritual gifts and ministerial callings, and no one can manipulate the way in which God chooses to utilize individuals in ministry. The sole purpose of such spiritual gifts and callings is to edify the Body of Christ (Church) and simultaneously bring glory to Christ, who is the head of the Church.

It is imperative for persons whom God singles out to exemplify a life above reproach. In other words, they must come to appreciate and adhere to a life of holiness.

Simply stated, no one should get the *big head,* but rather each of us should always display a spirit of thanksgiving and humility. Because God has purposed for each of us to fulfill a heavenly purpose, each of us must be open to receiving his or her assignment. Perhaps this Chinese proverb will help you understand how important it is to be opened to what you are supposed to do. The proverb says, *"Tell me something and I will forget. Show me something and I will remember. Involve me and I will understand."* Your gifts and calling are profound examples of how

God expects believers to come together both spiritually and socially, in order to establish a more wholesome environment.

I hope that you are as inspired and blessed reading this book as I have been in researching, compiling and sharing this pertinent information. This book can be studied personally or collectively as a study guide, manual, course, and teaching tool. It is my prayer that you will soon discover and come to appreciate God's amazing and profound methods of selection and the wide array of persons He utilizes to fulfill His will.

By and large, I have selected the *Revised Standard Version* for all scriptural references. In addition, I draw definitions and explanations of Biblical terms and phrases from *Vine's Complete Expository Dictionary of Old and New Testament Words,* by W.E. Vine, Merrill F. Unger, and William White, Jr.

Course Outline

I.   What is a Gift?
II.   What is a Calling?
III.   What is the Anointing?
IV.   Mission of the Holy Spirit in the life of the Church
V.   Spiritual Gifts in the life of the Church

1. Administrative Gifts (Ephesians 4:11)
   a. Apostles
   b. Prophets
   c. Evangelists
   d. Pastors
   e. Teachers
2. Supportive or Motivational Gifts (Romans 12:3-8)
   a. Prophecy
   b. Service
   c. Teaching
   d. Exhortation
   e. Giving
   f. Administration
   g. Mercy
3. Extraordinary Gifts (1 Corinthians 12:4-11)
   a. Word of Wisdom
   b. Word of Knowledge
   c. Gift of Faith
   d. Gift of Healing
   e. Working of Miracles
   f. Prophesy
   g. Discernment of Spirits
   h. Unknown Tongues
   i. Interpretation of Tongues
4. Church Leadership (1 Corinthians 12:28)
   a. Apostles
   b. Prophets
   c. Teachers
   d. Workers of Miracles
   e. Healers
   f. Helpers
   g. Administrators
   h. Speakers in various kinds of tongues

VI. Examples of Biblical characters cooperating and resisting their calling:
1. Adam
2. Noah
3. Joseph
4. Abraham
5. Moses
6. Gideon
7. Deborah
8. Elijah
9. Ruth
10. Samuel
11. Saul
12. David
13. Solomon
14. Isaiah
15. Ezekiel
16. Jeremiah
17. Jonah
18. Job
19. Mary
20. John the Baptist
21. Peter
22. James
23. John
24. Judas
25. Phillip
26. Apollos
27. Dorcas
28. Timothy
29. Barnabas
30. Silas
31. Ananias & Sapphira
32. Paul
33. Jesus Christ

VII. Practical Guidelines and Virtues for Effective Ministry
1. A life of holiness
2. Humility
3. Patience
4. Effective communication (oral and written skills)
5. Devotion (prayer, fasting, study, praise and meditation)
6. Willingness to serve

Chapter 1

What is a Gift?

Perhaps this little story will help open our hearts and minds to the true meaning surrounding gifts and giving. The story is told about a rich man giving a million dollars to a local congregation. Once the offering was given he paused to see if the pastor would recognize his generous donation before the congregation.

Upon observing that the pastor was not going to recognize his donation the man paused and said, "You could have at least said, 'Thank you.' "

The pastor replied, "He who gives should be thankful that he has to give."

Drawing from this story, we are compelled to ponder the following questions: Why do we give gifts? What compels us to act?

The term *gift* is commonly used in all societies around the world, both today as was in the biblical era. The New Testament Greek language introduces seven words pertaining to gifts, expounding a wide range of meanings. Let me share a couple of them. The Greek term *doron* denotes a gift being presented as an expression of honor (Mt 2:11), or support of the temple and the needs of the poor (Mt 15:5, Mk 7:11; Lk 21:1, 4). This term also refers to a sacrificial offering.

Another Greek term *dorea,* denotes a free gift, stressing gratuitous character (Acts 2:28, 8:20; Rom 5:17). Yet, there appears to be a consistent thread in these definitions, which suggests that gifts and the act of giving encompass the spirit of grace, mercy, love, and a free will.

Universally and historically speaking, we must always remember that the philosophy and nature of gifts and giving carry with them the element of surprise, wherein something of value is freely disbursed without any knowledge on the part of the one receiving the gift until it is presented to them. Expressed another way, no one earned or expected a gift. Gifts usually originated from a higher source or official, and were disbursed to someone who was in need. However, this is not necessarily so in all cases.

Whenever we see the display and distribution of gifts in the faith community they serve as tangible and concrete examples of God's grace, mercy and kindness, as well as His approach for addressing a specific need. Comparably, we should remain faithful to the true meaning and origin of gifts when we present them. And by all means, we should avoid giving senseless gifts.

For example, in reference to the annual African American non-heroic celebration called *Kwanzaa*, Dr. R. Maulana Karenga encourages the community at large to participate in a seven-day celebration. During this period, adults are encouraged to give gifts, zawadi (Ki-Swahili term) to children. According to custom, each gift should always reflect something pertaining to African culture, and they also should encourage the exchange in order to promote knowledge. Hence, the principle of giving expressed in Kwanzaa emphasizes the significance of the gifts, as opposed to the mere obsession over material possessions.

Remember that while no one merits a gift, the act of giving is essential to helping to bring the best out of our character. The giver is expected to give unselfishly and with a sense of purpose, while the receiver of any gift is expected to display humility and gratitude to the presenter. This sentiment is expressed in an African proverb which says, *"Being grateful, a man makes himself deserving of yet another kindness."*

Notes

Chapter 2

What is a Calling?

The Old Testament Hebrew term *qara* refers to a calling out or summoning by an official entity and the specification of a name (Gen 1:5). A call is a summons or declaration and may include the following: specific task (Isa 65:12); to petition God for aid (Gen 4:26); to call out loudly (Job 5:11, 1 Sam 17:8); to proclaim (Ex 32:5).

Nonetheless, the call of God always permeates around a specific assignment that usually propels or thrusts the individual into some form of public ministry. A spiritual calling is somewhat like a fire burning in someone's heart and a message of truth and reconciliation disbursed from their lips. There are many aspects of a calling. On one hand, the Church, a spiritual corporate body is described as a *Called Out Assembly.* Her nature is grounded in holiness and destined to give glory to Christ (1 Peter 1:13-17).

Comparably, God also singles out and calls individuals into ministry, those whom He has predestined to provide some type of leadership on behalf of the Church (See Rom 8:29-30; 2 Thes 1:11-12: Col 1:24-29;) God always empowers such individuals with spiritual gifts. In light of this truism, notice how Paul admonished Timothy to remain active with his gift. (2 Tim 1:6-9). Putting it another way, it is certain that anyone who is called to ministry will also have a spiritual mandate to emerge from the crowd and declare or proclaim the Gospel of the Kingdom via one or more of the offices of Apostle, Prophet, Evangelist, Pastor and Teacher. While these administrative gifts are clearly earmarked, this does not exhaust the manner by which God may call individuals to serve in different areas of ministry. Please do not confuse ecclesiastical or congregational appointments with a heavenly calling. A heavenly calling is God's divine invitation into leadership.

Apostle Paul shed some light for those whom God has called. He said, "We know that in everything God works for good with those who love him, who are called according to his purpose." (Rom 8:28) Challenges and adversities are inevitable, but the purpose and intent of God will be fulfilled through the faithful witness. In other words God always knows the course of the righteous. He supplies adequate provision—seen or unseen, along the way—so that in the end, those whom He has called will look back and thank Him for the experience. It is all for your good.

In the New Testament, we are presented with a variety of Greek verbs and nouns relating to a divine callling. For example, the Greek verb *kaleo* refers to an invitation to share in blessings of redemption (Rom 8:30; 1 Cor 1:9; 1 Thes 2:12). It may also refer to a vocation or destination.

The Greek noun *klesis* denotes a calling in regards to a heavenly origin, nature and destiny (Phil 3:14; Rom 11:29; Eph 1:18). For additional meanings and references, please refer to *Vine's Complete Expository Dictionary of Old and New Testament Words.*

In these lessons, we will explore the Biblical or theological mandates, those unique ways and purposes that are associated with an individual calling. You should also note that a calling is an appeal and the singling out of an individual or group of people in order to personify a life of holiness in the midst of an unrighteous environment. By no means should we forget that these callings have a spiritual mandate to admonish the righteous and proclaim a message of condemnation against all unrighteousness. Please be mindful that individuals are called to serve God in spite of their human frailties, faults or lack of experience because God is the master of reshaping their character. Thus our calling to ministry is the epitome of what I call *on-the-job training* because God develops each of us as we submit in obedience to the calling.

Some time ago, a friend sent me this information pertaining to Biblical characters (See details in later chapter) entitled *"God Can Use You."* So, the next time you feel like God can't use you, just remember…

- **Noah** was a drunk
- **Abraham** was too old
- **Isaac** was a daydreamer
- **Jacob** was a liar
- **Leah** was ugly
- **Joseph** was abused
- **Moses** couldn't talk
- **Gideon** was afraid
- **Samson** had long hair, and was a womanizer
- **Rahab** was a prostitute
- **Jeremiah and Timothy** were too young
- **David** had an affair and was a murderer
- **Elijah** was suicidal
- **Isaiah** preached naked
- **Jonah** ran from God
- **Naomi** was a widow
- **Job** went bankrupt

- **John the Baptist** ate bugs
- **Peter** denied Christ
- **The Disciples** fell asleep while praying
- **Martha** worried about everything
- **Mary Magdalene** was demon possessed
- **The Samaritan Woman** was divorced more than once
- **Zaccheus** was too small
- **Paul** was too religious and a persecutor of Christians
- **Lazarus** was dead

Please no more excuses;
God is waiting to use your full potential

Chapter 3
What is the Anointing?

In recent years, the term *anointing* has been widely and loosely used throughout the Church. In my humble opinion, however, it appears that a substantial part of the faith community (leaders and laity) has yet to be adequately taught about the full implication of this term whereas they do not fully appreciate or even understand its meaning and usage.

For starters, we must clearly understand that God anoints individuals to fulfill services on behalf of His kingdom. As such, an anointed individual should always be both *mission oriented* and *purpose driven,* because his or her anointing is ordained for the chief purpose of bringing glory to the Most High God or Jesus Christ, as the Son of God. Hence, the anointing takes on great significance, especially when there has been a deviation from righteousness within the covenant community.

Secondly, we should recognize that emotional gestures and extraordinary capabilities might be associated with the anointing. However we must never lose sight of the mission and purpose that God has assigned to the individual. And we should always remember that an anointing is not for the edification of the individual, but is specifically for the edification of God. It is for this reason that God anoints individuals whom others would least expect to be singled out—so that there will be no doubt that God is in control. We can see this principle illustrated in God's selection of a Persian king named Cyrus to liberate the Children of Israel, even though the king was not a member of the covenant community (Isa 45). Simply stated, the *why* is always more important than *who, what and how*. There will always be favorable results and deliverance when the anointed one faithfully carries out his or her assignment.

Thirdly, an anointing is always associated with the *Messianic Kingdom,* which portrays the role in which Christ spiritually orchestrates and reconciles us back to the Father. Historically and Biblically, there were three unique offices or titles associated with the anointing:

> *Priest:* The Hebrew term *Kohen* denotes priest. This individual served as an authorized and anointed official who mediated and offered sacrifices on behalf of the community at the altar. In addition, the priest had a mandate to teach the Law.

> *Prophet:* The Hebrew term *Nabi* refers to a prophet. These anointed messengers fervently expressed and articulated the oracles of God primarily to the faith community, but at times

they spoke against other nations. They foretold the future, while at the same time challenged the community to live righteously. They had a mandate to teach the Law.

King: The Hebrew term *Melek* refers to a king. This person served as the anointed sovereign ruler and was expected to exemplify justice and mercy, while at the same time display a regal and royal disposition. The king, like the priest and prophet, also had a mandate to teach the Law.

Individuals entering these highly esteemed offices were expected to personify righteousness, faith, love, and holiness at all times before God and the people.

Now, we can move forward to examining the biblical etymology of this term in both the Old and New Testaments.

The Old Testament term *masah* means anointing, smearing and consecrating. Typically, oil (but not always) was smeared on a person or object, thus transforming that entity into a sacred or holy vessel. See the following examples in the Old Testament: Gen 31:31; Lev 4:3, 5, 16; Jer 22:14; 1 Kings 19:16; 1 Sam 16:12; 1 Kings 1:39; Ex 30:22-25; Ps 2:2, 18:50).

The New Testament introduces a variety of terms that are related to *anointing.* Perhaps, the most familiar word is *Christos.* This term denotes Messiah (the anointed one with oil) and the Son of God who was sent to earth as the official messenger of the Kingdom of God. There are numerous scriptures depicting this title and office i.e., Mt 2:4; Acts 2;31; Mk 14:61-61; Jn 5:6; 1 Cor 3:11; Eph 3:17; Gal 3:20.

In the context of the entire Bible, we observe individuals or objects being anointed in order to fulfill various goals or purposes. In the scope of our discussion, however, we will focus only on the individual being singled out by God for the sole purpose of declaring a message of reconciliation or condemnation against unrighteousness. In that capacity, the anointed individual becomes an empowered spiritual agent for a time and season. But, please be cognizant and remember that this is not an emotional or romanticized term, but rather it denotes an active and faithful witness whom God has selected to act on behalf of the Kingdom of God.

In order to drive home these concepts let me share a few comments on a related term, *chosen.* In the process, we will examine the etymology of the term along with some supporting scriptures, all because I want to accentuate the fact that chosen individuals are anointed to do kingdom ministry.

In the Old Testament, the Hebrew word *bahir* refers to chosen ones, and the term *bahar* deals with choosing. In the New Testament, the Greek term *eklego* denotes to pick out or select. For the purpose of this discussion, we will examine a couple of New Testament scriptures that might better help us understand the spiritual mandate associated with being chosen.

First, let us look at the ending of Jesus' parable entitled *The Wedding Feast* (Mt 22:2-14). "For many are called, but few are chosen." The initial invited guests were probably friends and family who were extended an opportunity to attend the feast. But instead of graciously accepting the invitation, each one of them refused (they represented the called ones). Even though the called ones made excuses and rejected the call, the story continues, illustrating the notion that God will neither be denied nor embarrassed.

The parable goes on to report that another pool of invited guests was summoned, comprising a group of individuals who we would have least expected to attend. Nonetheless there was a certain man from the latter pool of invitees who accepted the invitation to attend the feast, but failed to dress properly. In this instance, the improperly dressed man was actually chosen to be in a favorable place, but his improper attire caused him to be dispelled. Hence, we can discern from this parable that chosen individuals come with an anointing and they are expected to behave and look a certain way.

The second scripture is found in 1 Peter 2:9-10: "But you are a chosen race, a royal priesthood, a holy nation, God's own people, that you may declare the wonderful deeds of him who called you out of darkness into his marvelous light. Once you were no people but now you are God's people; once you had not received mercy but now you have received mercy." This text articulates our significance and function, for each believer is both chosen and anointed with a specific purpose and mission.

A closing remark and thought for the reader to ponder: Because the nature and essence of God is holy, He has called and chosen a group of people from all walks of life (Jews and Gentiles) to reflect His character, i.e. worship and service. Both the individual and corporate body must come together and reflect the very nature and mannerism of God.

Notes

Chapter 4

Mission of the Holy Spirit in the Church

What is the Church? The Church is a spiritual entity or living organism comprised of individual beings that accept the sovereignty of God and simultaneously adhere to the life and teachings of Jesus Christ during this current dispensation that we call *grace*. The New Testament servess as a compilation of the teachings of Jesus, the proclamation of the gospel and the doctrines of the church. Listed is an overview of the books therein: Gospels (4); History of the Church, memorialized as the Acts of the Apostles (1); and the Epistles or Letters (22). Generally speaking, each of these twenty-seven books clearly points to the Kingdom of God, as well as to the mandate of the Church in interacting with and governing this temporal world in which we live.

Jesus came proclaiming this profound and eternal message, as recorded throughout the Gospels (i.e. Mk 1:14f). It is important to note that while the scriptures reveal that the Church was conceived in the mind of heart of Jesus beforehand (Mt 16:18), the Church was not born or birthed until we saw the Pentecostal experience in Jerusalem according to the scripture (Acts 2).

Since the *Day of Pentecost,* the Holy Spirit has been freely disbursed and made available for everyone to receive should they acknowledge Jesus Christ as the Son of God. Jesus really wanted us to understand the relevance of the Holy Spirit. That is why He shed considerable light on this subject prior to His departure, as recorded in the Gospel of John, Chapter 14.

During Jesus' earthly ministry He was the counselor, *Paraclete* (Greek term) and the manifestation of God. However, since His ascension, the Holy Spirit has becomes the unseen presence and official agent of the Holy One (Godhead) whereby deliverance is seen (Lk 4:16-21) and fellowship is created (Acts 2:43-47) within the faith community.

The Holy Spirit is described in diverse manners throughout the New Testament. For example, the scriptures refer to the Holy Spirit as the Holy Ghost, Guide, Teacher, New Wine, Discerner, Comforter, Spirit of Truth, Fire, Outpouring, Healer, and Baptizer, etc.

However, Jesus passionately referred to the Holy Spirit as the *Spirit of Truth,* simply because the Church or religion as a whole can easily be infiltrated and influenced by the *Spirit of Error.* The Holy Spirit always bears witness to Jesus Christ, just as we have observed, the Son of God consistently testify and honor His Father. The Holy Spirit is a faithful witness, and so should the Body of Christ should be likewise.

The Holy Spirit empowers the believer to live a saved and sanctified life, while overcoming all the onslaughts or adversities of a sinful world. Being baptized and filled with the Holy Spirit, the believer becomes better equipped to understand the mysteries or hidden ways of God.

The Holy Spirit is animated and active. Therefore, we will see various reactions i.e. speaking in tongues, slaying in the spirit, prophetic utterance, dancing, and praying. However, I want to caution you to become disciplined in the spirit, because Satan delights in emotions, music, noise, and distractions.

In a letter written to the Corinthian Church, Apostle Paul provides sound doctrines regarding the operation of the Holy Spirit within the life of the Church in a letter written to the Corinthian Church. (Read 1 Corinthians, Chapters 12 through 14). After discussing the manner in which the Holy Spirit ought to function in the Church as opposed to the disorder commonly seen in the Church, Paul concluded, "Let all things be done decently and in order." (1 Cor 14:40).

Notes

Chapter 5

Spiritual Gifts in the Life of the Church

Scriptures: Matthew 16:18; Romans 12:6; 16:1-21; 1 Peter 4:10; 1 Timothy 4:14; Ephesians 4:11-12; 1 Corinthians 12:7-10; John 14:11-12; Acts 8:5-7; Acts 11:15-18; 15:25-29; 16:1-7 etc.

Origin of the Church

While engaged in a conversation with His disciples, Jesus brought a newfound meaning and understanding to the mission of the church. Heretofore, the Grecian community interpreted the role of the church as a political, rather than a spiritual entity because Jesus talked about *establishing* an entity made countless references to a *kingdom* in the course of his teachings. However, after Jesus' revelation to Peter and the other disciples, she (the Church) becomes spiritual in nature and destined to bring glory to Christ. She is mandated to grow, evangelize and penetrate the global community.

She is called or summoned to a life of righteousness and holiness because of the redemptive act of Jesus Christ. Let me introduce a few terms biblical historical terms that might assist us in understanding the role of the Church. The New Testament Greek term *Ekklesia*, denotes a called out assembly or body of believers with a kindred spirit and shares in a common destiny. The Church is the community of faith, which adheres to the life and teachings of Jesus Christ. She is similar to the Old Testament covenant community called Israel.

The Old Testament term *Qahal* refers to an assembly, while the term *Qoheleth* has to do with the speaker or preacher. In other words the called out community needs to have anointed men and women who are skilled in the scripture, so that they might proclaim the message of the Kingdom of God. Both Israel and the Church represent the glory of God and gifts and calling are distributed in order to serve the Assembly of God.

Thus the Church is depicted in various endearing terms or phrases i.e. Bride of Christ, Temple of God, Family of God, Household of Faith, Beloved and Little Children etc. Your gifts and callings must edify the Church while at the same time bring glory to Jesus Christ, otherwise you are operating under the influence of Satan.

Spiritual Gifts

The term *spiritual* refers to being alive or animated. According to the mind and purpose of God, the essence of life or their nature is profoundly expressed and personified through human beings or being made aware of Ultimate Concerns versus temporal matters.

A present or the act of sharing something with another is called a gift. The New Testament term *charisma* is Greek in origin and denotes *spiritual gifts* (James 1:17) or *gifts of grace.* These gifts are selectively given to members of the Church so that glory might be rendered unto Christ and the body might receive edification.

The term *grace* refers to unmerited favor; merciful. Grace is the ability and the wherewithal of God to act on behalf of a sinning community, within a time frame (dispensation), so that we might experience reconciliation. In short, I see grace as the window of opportunity extended by God in order for us to realize the paramount value of a holy life.

Shortly I want to share with you several categories of spiritual gifts presented by the Apostle Paul in the New Testament Church. However, I want to caution you that everyone empowered with administrative or leadership gifts are definitely called to ministry. However, persons with extraordinary and motivational gifts may or may not be called in a technical sense. In either case, your gifts may be boldly or openly displayed, or quietly carried out with little or no attention drawn to you.

For example, the hands, tongue, nose, ears and eyes are part of what we commonly call the five senses. These organs are integral members of our body and they are easily seen and recognized. However, there are other organs or members of the same body that are not prominently or visibly displayed i.e. blood, lungs, liver, bones and heart in a manner like we see the five senses. This analysis is very important because, the truth is they are equally important if we want to have a healthy body. All spiritual gifts are important to the body of Christ, even though some may get more attention than others.

For example, there is an old cliché circulating in the Church circles, which says, *"I am just a bench member."* There is no way an individual can be saved and truly love Christ and think they do not have a gift or calling assigned to them. The spirit of Satan permeates around idleness, criticism, excuse making, rebellion and separation; however, we must rebuke this spirit at all costs and not tolerate it in our ministry. The Church must remain vibrant and in order for this to happen she needs the full participation and cooperation of every member.

Now, let us look at several illustrations and categories of spiritual gifts that reflect men and women whom God singled out and called them to these esteemed offices. Please take note these are not religious or organizational appointments, but rather anointed position. The vibrant, animated and glorious spirit of the Church is contingent upon men and women who will be faithful to their gifts and callings. Please take note the gift of prophecy is listed in every category, and rightfully so. This gift serves as a constant reminder the church family needs to overcome a wayward spirit or disobedience to the truth.

Administrative Gifts (Ephesians 4:11-12).

It is critical for the Church to acknowledge and allow each one of these distinguished and esteemed gifts to operate without prejudice or interference. Apostles and Pastors tend to get more attention and recognition in the life of the Church than the other administrators. However, need I remind you the most celebrated and recognized clergy in America for the past 60 years is Billy Graham? Mr. Graham, as he is affectionately called, is neither an Apostle nor Pastor. Instead, he humbly accepted his calling as an evangelist, cultivated the gift and the rest is history. Each gift must be respected, cultivated and operated in the life of the church just as you would be impressed with a secular organization displaying a variety of administrators and vice-presidents working cooperatively and effectively.

Therefore, I strongly admonish persons called and anointed with either of these gifts to organize spiritually and legally. By and large, the Apostles and Pastors tend to be well organized but I want to challenge the prophets, evangelist and teachers to do likewise.

Apostles: Commissioned to organize, oversee and establish churches in spiritually undeveloped areas, while at the same time administering over areas already established; chief administrator and overseer who serve over a vast area. Please do not confuse this office with a Bishop, because they are appointed.

Prophets: Fierce messengers of God, who pronounce judgment for the future, rebuke and admonish the community of faith to live righteously; declare the oracles of God.

Evangelists: A person who proclaims the gospel with a fervent spirit; spread the good news of the Kingdom of God like a flaming fire.

Pastors: A person who displays a shepherding spirit; to continuously nourish and protects the flock of God; display compassion.

Teachers: This person is closely aligned with the role of a pastor. A person who analyzes, present and clarifies the doctrines of the Church.

Supportive or Motivational Gifts *(Romans 12:3-8)*

These gifts should not be confused with the administrative or leadership gifts. I like to liken these gifts to the hidden organs in the human body or nuts and bolts that keep a structure together. Motivational gifts are designed to keep us charged up with an upbeat spirit. Another way of looking at these gifts can be seen through the role of the ground crew at the airport. The pilot and stewardess may be thrust in the forefront but the public knows who really keep the industry flowing. Be thankful for your gift and do your best for the glory of Christ and we will see a vibrant Church.

Prophesy: Displays the ability to express the word of God in a stirring manner primarily to the covenant community so that we will see results i.e., corrections or judgments.

Serving: Ability to show love by unselfishly and practically attending to the needs of others.

Teaching: Ability to clarify and articulate the truth or doctrines expressed in the scriptures.

Exhortation: Ability to encourage and admonish others to grow spiritually i.e., praise, worship, testimony etc.

Giving: Ability to contribute generously of their time and resources in order to fulfill the spiritual mandates of the Church.

Administration: Ability to coordinate and organize the affairs i.e., ministries and auxiliaries of the church.

Mercy: Ability to identify and tend to those who are in dire need or distress.

Notes

Extraordinary Gifts (1 Corinthians 12:4-11)

This is a very unique grouping of gifts, but nonetheless they are equally important to the life of the church. Some may call these individuals strange or mystical. For some strange reason, they are in touch with the spirit in such a way they must be viewed as spiritual enablers who help sharpen and encourage both individuals and the corporate body to overcome adversities in the strength of the Lord. Once again, they may not necessarily be out front, but they are the spiritual technicians or specialists that aid in spiritual repairing and renewal during critical junctures of our lives.

Word of Wisdom: The ability to impart insightful spiritual truths to another during an awkward time (James 3:13-18); to speak soundly and truthfully.

Word of Knowledge: The ability to search and know the scriptures and provide pertinent or precise information to another about a specific concern within the Church family.

Gift of Faith: Person who models their life after Abraham (Gen 12:1f); to wholeheartedly believe and follow Christ, even when it goes against the conventional wisdom of the group.

Gift of Healing: To be empowered to pronounce healing both physically and spiritually, such as laying on hands and speaking deliverance into existence.

Working of Miracles: Allowing the marvelous and wonderful acts of God to invade the human experiences and cause something to occur that otherwise cannot be readily explained.

Prophesy: Speaking on behalf of God in a corrective manner, or in order to avoid judgments.

Discernment of Spirits: The ability to distinguish the Spirit of Truth from the Spirit of Error within the lives of others in the Church.

Unknown Tongues: A special gift to the believer that results in uttering an unfamiliar language (Acts 2:1-4; 10:46; 19:6). These tongues serve as praise to God and a sign to unbelievers (1 Cor 14:22). This seems to be a gift that is extended to all believers who have accepted Christ as their personal Savior. The gift may be unknown to the one who is speaking, but the language may be known to someone else. The gift is clearly demonstrated without rehearsing.

Interpretation of Tongues: Another special gift that ought not to be confused with the previous one. Aside from the Unknown Tongues, God has equipped certain believers with the ability to explain or interpret what is being said (1 Cor 14:13f).

Church Leadership (1 Corinthians 12:28)

Take note this is a variation or alternative outline of leaders in the Church similar to what we saw previously in the Ephesians congregation i.e. apostles, prophets and teachers (Eph 4:11). However, there seems to be several other gifts that may not come under the motivational or extraordinary gifts. Therefore, we must treat these gifts as esteemed spiritual administrators, and whenever there is a reference to leadership this is a clear indication of spiritual authority and organization. I will share a few comments on each of these gifts and callings, but please observe there is a consistent pattern wherein the Apostles and Prophets are always listed first and second.

Apostles: They serve as chief administrators over the flock of God (see earlier remarks). Another way of looking at their role is to take a look at the strongest and anchoring finger on the hand called the thumb.

Prophets: Generally speaking, if you want to emphasize a point or really get someone's attention you would use this finger called the index or pointer finger. Likewise, prophesy is designed to stir the spirit and get one's attention primarily in the faith community, while at the same time they may be called upon to deliver oracles against the unrighteous.

Teachers: This gift is extremely important, because they are expected to expound and analyze the tenets and doctrines of the faith via practical and concrete illustrations. The Parables of the Kingdom serve as an exemplary model for all teachers. Teachers must be creative, inspiring and well organized at all times. I would like to refer to this gift as the little finger on the hand.

Workers of Miracles: Once again, this gift is given to selected individuals whereby they clearly help demonstrate the phenomenal manner in which God interrupts the normal course of events in order to meet a need as well as cause individuals to become followers of Christ.

Gift of Healing: Every generation seems to be confronted with a variety of illnesses, just like we saw during the Biblical era. Therefore, this gift is uniquely distributed to individuals in order for them to rebuke sickness and disease in order for the person delivered as well as those surrounding to give glory unto Christ.

Helpers: The Mission of the Church was clearly defined by Jesus (Lk 4:18-19; Mt 25:31-46). In order to fulfill the spiritual mandate of the Church, there must be individuals filled with kindness, mercy and compassion for the disinherited or *"the least of these among us."* We must be sensitive to those within and without the faith community and do all we can to aide in transforming these distasteful realities (Gal 6:10).

Administrators: The Church is a living organism with many members. Therefore, she must be organized in order to address both the spiritual and legal (or civic) requirements. She must allow creative thinkers and administrators express themselves in order to make sure the business of ministry is in order at all times.

Speakers in various kinds of tongues: Aside from the unknown tongues, there are individuals God has gifted with the ability to pray, sing and praise God via the spirit in such a way that their languages are diverse and only God knows what they are saying.

The Church remains a mystery to the world, but to the body of Baptized Believers, she is a spiritual vehicle under the auspice of the *Kingdom of God*. The temporal world will end as we know her, but the Church will live perpetually. She will be ushered into the glorious presence of God according to our faith in Jesus Christ.

The Church provides both shelter and fulfillment for all those who embrace her. She is greater than any culture, denomination, ritual or tradition (although we may see all of them creatively expressed therein). She is alive and doing well in this present age. However, she must always safeguard against religiosity, personality clashes, self-righteousness and denominationalism, because they tend to upstage the glorious Christ and give her a bad name.

Therefore, I admonish you to remain humble and obedient to the Holy Spirit. The spiritual gifts are freely disbursed to help build up the Body of Christ and not individual egos or personalities. The more we allow the gifts to operate in the ministry then the less confusion we will see. I have tried to demonstrate in practical terms the various gifts at different levels, because I want to make it very clear that everyone has a role in the Church. Please discover your gift and do not covet my gift or another.

Notes

Chapter 6
Examples of Biblical Characters Accepting
and Resisting their Calling

Stories have a unique way of opening our mind and heart to the truth. Therefore, this reminds me of the story I heard about the scorpion and the turtle preparing to cross a river.

The scorpion was not known to be a good swimmer, so he said to the turtle, "Do you mind letting me ride on your back across the river?"

The turtle said, "If I allow you to ride on my back you will bite me."

The scorpion replied, "Now, that is not logical, because if I bite you both of us will drown."

The two of them reached an agreement and they started across the river. About midway the scorpion bit the turtle.

The turtle said, "May I ask you a question before the two of us drowns?"

"Why did you bite me after telling me it was not logical to do so?"

The scorpion said, "It has nothing to do with logic. It has everything to do with my character."

Watch the character of a person and that will explain their behavior, whether good or bad. Since God's character is holy it is His intent to shape our character into holy vessels.

In this lesson, I want to share practical illustrations about selected Biblical characters and give insights in the way these individuals cooperated and rebelled regarding their gifts and callings. We tend to romanticize these men and women by trying to make them larger than life or as if they always did what was correct, without examining the scriptures and recognize their human frailties.

In order to really appreciate what God did through them I want to suggest we put forth several questions as a format to learn as much as we can from their experiences with God and the community they were assigned to minister. In so doing, you should begin to dramatically minimize your mistakes. The questions are as follows:

1. Where can we find this character in the Bible?
2. Where did they come from, and what do we know about their environment?
3. What was their mission or purpose?
4. How were they called or what gifts did they display?
5. What about their strengths and weaknesses?
6. What can we learn from them?

Adam

The story of Adam is found in the second through fifth chapters of Genesis. Adam represents the first man created in the image and likeness of the Most High God (Holy). He was created in the mind of God but shaped from mother earth, while at the same time God gave him the ability to make choices. Adam, along with his wife Eve, was created to worship God and maintain the Garden of Eden.

Eden or the *Garden of God* is geographically described as a tropical place in the east. And in my humble opinion that place was in East Africa, the *Motherland*. Adam's call and assignment was connected to being created as an eternal being (Gen 2:4-25). This creative energy was exemplified in his ability to assign names to other created beings as well as have dominion over the earth and all the inhabitants. Adam's weakness is linked to curiosity and disobedience to God's unambiguous instruction. We must take heed and observe how this utopia and blissful place was replaced with trouble and death, due to curiosity and rebellion—or the influence of that scoundrel, Satan.

Noah

We recount the story of Noah in the fifth through ninth chapters of Genesis. Noah is the son of Lamech. The precise modern geographical location of the story is uncertain, but we clearly understand that Noah lived during an adulterous, thrill-seeking and rebellious era. His mission was to proclaim a message of repentance (Gen 6:5-8) and to build an ark in order to save his household from the eminent cataclysmic flood (Gen 6:13-22).

Noah displayed a spirit of humility, obedience and patience. And he embraced a life of righteousness (Gen 6:8; 7:1-10). Despite his noteworthy qualities though, after the flood Noah showed weakness by getting drunk, speaking out of character, and allegedly putting a curse on his grandson, Canaan.

Each one of us should appreciate this story and the various lessons therein. For we must not allow ourselves to be put in a drunken or spiritual stupor that may cause reproach before God and those whom we represent in the community. Noah was called by God, and he remained a model in scripture. But remember, *"Noah was drunk"* (Gen 9:21), yet God used him.

Joseph

This is no doubt, one of the most colorful characters in the entire Bible. The saga of Joseph is found in Genesis, chapters 37 through 50. Joseph is one of two sons born to the union of Jacob and Rachel (Gen 35:24). However, he is the eleventh son of Jacob (Gen 35:22-26). It appears that Joseph was born near Bethlehem or Ephrath, which is in Canaan (Gen 35:16-29).

Joseph's mission was to overcome a series of adversities, which were clearly orchestrated by God, in order for him to later be positioned to save his family and others from death (Gen 35:5-11). His gift and calling revolved around having and interpreting dreams. And while Joseph's dreams clearly got him into trouble with his brothers, his gift as a dreamer also later caused him to be released from prison and brought to the house of Pharaoh to be promoted to second in command over Egypt (Gen 41).

Joseph showed strength and integrity in the face of temptations and adversities (Gen 39:7-23). However, his weakness caused him to speak both premature and immaturely among his brothers. Yet, at the same time, God seems to allow adversities and challenges in our lives in order to develop our character.

We should learn from Joseph's story that while we may be aware of our gifts and callings, the times or seasons for them to manifest may be much later. And while you may wear the *coat of many colors* and display the gift of a dreamer, always remember that not everyone will celebrate with you. *"As long as a man has a dream in his heart, he cannot lose the significance of living."* (Thurman) Joseph was used by God in an awesome way, but remember, *Joseph was abused* (Gen 37:18-28)

Abraham

The story of Abraham can be found in the eleventh through twenty-fifth chapters of Genesis. Chronologically, Abraham comes before Joseph. But, here, I chose to do otherwise because, in my humble opinion, this character servess as the spiritual progenitor of nation builders.

A careful study of the scriptures reveals to us that Abraham may have played a more significant role than Adam. Furthermore, I am convinced that Abraham and David are the most prominent biblical characters prior to the coming of Jesus Christ. The name Abram denotes father, and Abraham refers to anointed father. He is called the first Haribu (Hebrew). He is the son of Terah, and their ancestral home was Ur of Chaldea (modern day Iraq).

Abram (Abraham) was summoned to enter into a covenant with the Most High God even though he had no prior relationship with this deity (Gen 12). Yahweh instructed Abram to depart from his comfort zone and go to a place pre-ordained for those future generations who would adhere to a life of righteousness. Abram's mission was to personify a life of faith and righteousness. His wife, Sarai (Sarah) and he were given a mandate to bring forth a son even though they were beyond the child-bearing years. (Gen 15)

Abram is definitely a model, but when faced with a challenge he opted to lie. (Gen 12:10-20) Nonetheless, due to God's favor things worked out on his behalf. And on another occasion, Abram allowed Sarai and Hagar (Gen 16) to cause him to display poor judgment via a carnal plan. Still despite such flaws, Abraham is called the *Friend of God* and the *Father of the Faith*. His name and character is revered in Judaism, Christianity and Islam.

Indeed, it is because of Abraham that we have come to learn that family and traditions, experience, age, and diverse challenges all seem to be in the spiritual mixing bowl of being called. And while Christians, Jews and Muslims all revere him, let us not forget that Abraham *was too old* (Gen 17:1).

Moses

The story of Moses is found in the chapters between Exodus 2 through Deuteronomy 34. It is perhaps the longest saga in the foundational books of the Old Testament (Torah). Moses was a Hebrew from the tribe of Levi (Ex 2:1-2, 10), but his name reflects the culture and influence of Egypt. He was born during the period of the Hebrew Israelites' sojourn in Egypt. He was summoned by God to leave Egypt and dwell in the Sinai Peninsula long enough until he experienced his rendezvous or encounters, called the *theophany* at Mt. Sinai (aka Mt. Horeb) with the Most High God. This eye-opening experience is commonly known as the *burning bush* (Ex 3).

Moses was singled out to confront Pharaoh about the affliction of the Hebrew Israelites and then lead them to the *Promised Land* (Ex 3:10). After a series of disasters launched against Egypt, God allow Moses to lead the *Children of Israel* into the wilderness, in order to teach and prepare them for the land promised to their father, Abraham.

Moses was a liberator, lawgiver and prophet (Num 12). His strength permeated around meekness (Num 12:3), organizational and conquering skills (Num 13), and intolerance for idolatry and disobedience (Num 16). Moses is by far one of the most esteemed characters in the Hebraic tradition, but please do not forget this reality: *Moses could not talk well* (Ex 4:10), yet God used him. Of all the prophets, only Moses and Elijah appeared later in history during the *Transfiguration of Christ* (Lk 9:28-36).

Gideon

The story of Gideon (Jg 6-8) takes place during the biblical era known as the *Judges.* This was a challenging time period for Israel because they had to overcome other nations' occupancy of Canaan, the land that God promised to them as the children of Abraham. This period is also marked by blatant disregard for holiness and the embracing of idolatry.

In the unfolding of the story, the Angel of the LORD summons Gideon as a *Mighty Man of Valor* to deliver his tribe, Manasseh, from the Midianites. Only after a series of tests does Gideon embrace his newfound faith and anointing, which empowers him to lead the faith community with victory through God's favor.

Gideon's weaknesses stemmed from his initial lack of confidence in overcoming his humble beginnings (Jg 6:15), as well as his succumbing to idolatry in the latter part of his life (Judges 8:24-27). His strength centers upon his acknowledgment of God as the true ruler of Israel (Judges 8:23). Most definitely, we can appreciate Gideon's courage displayed in accepting the challenge to lead his tribe, as well as his eventual evolving into a mighty man of valor. Despite his notoriety though, remember, *Gideon was afraid* (Judges 6:13).

Deborah

Deborah is one of the Judges, whom God anointed in light of the spirit of rebellion that was rampant in the covenant community. Her fascinating story is found in the fourth and fifth chapters of Judges. Deborah had the gift of prophecy (Judges 4:4), though she would be called upon to serve as a liberator and judge. She was married and a well-respected woman in Israel. She spoke to Barak, a military leader over several of the northern tribes and made it known that the Lord would give Israel victory through him over the Canaanites.

Deborah is referred to as the *Mother of Israel* (Judges 5:7) in the *Song of Deborah and Barak* (Judges 5), where she poetically recounts various aspects of God's deliverance on behalf of Israel. I do not see any disobedience or notable flaws in her character. She was faithful and radiant in her vocation and leadership as a judge and prophetess. She refused to let a male dominated culture muzzle her mouth from declaring the oracles of God.

Elijah

This major prophet is definitely one of my favorite biblical characters due to his mystical origin and bizarre behavior. His story is both colorful and unusual (1Kings 17:1-2; Kings 2:11), and it helps set the tone for the pre-literary prophets in Israel. The name Elijah means *God is Lord*. He simply appears on the scene in Northern Israel without any ancestral reference, and is given an awesome and challenging mandate, whereby God directed him to deliver an oracle of judgment against both King Ahab and Israel.

Elijah is one of the most revered Prophets in the entire Bible. God allowed a severe famine to occur in order to demonstrate who is the true sovereign God of Canaan, Yahweh or Baal. There are a series of miracles and confrontations with King Ahab, Jezebel and various prophets of Baal. Elijah seemed to understand the mentor and mentee relationship, because he trained Elisha to be a successor (1 Kings 19:19-21).

Only Elijah and Moses appear during the *Transfiguration* with Jesus and the disciples (Lk 9:28-36). Despite his significant contribution, we cannot ignore the reality that *Elijah was suicidal* (1 Kings 19:4-8) due to the threat made by Jezebel. We salute him as a faithful and courageous individual who reverenced God more than his awesome challenges and realities.

Ruth

The story of Ruth is relatively short, being only four chapters long. It is one of the most endearing and passionate illustrations of God reaching across cultural and ethnic barriers in order to demonstrate the all-inclusive nature of divine fulfillment. Ruth is a Moabite, a legendary enemy of Israel. Yet God allowed her to marry a Hebrew, thus positioning her to be in the bloodline of Jesus Christ (Mt 1:5).

The calling of Ruth unfolds with a series of unpleasant experiences i.e. death of her husband (Ruth 1:5), departure from her ancestral homeland (Ruth 1:19), gleaning the field to sustain Naomi (mother-in-law) and herself. Her plight thus captured the attention of Boaz, a wealthy kinsman of Naomi. Ruth's mission was to help redeem the abandoned land of Naomi's family and marry Boaz.

As with Deborah, I cannot detect any weakness in the character of Ruth once she embraced a life of holiness. We are blessed to have this story preserved so that we may see how God clearly reaches across racial barriers to include those whom many would least expect. *Both Naomi and Ruth were widows*, but yet God used them to reclaim an inheritance.

Samuel

The story surrounding the call and ministry of Samuel (1 Samuel, Chapters 1-25) is by far one of the longest and most fascinating accounts in the Old Testament. The name Samuel basically means *Name of God.* His parents seem to have had limited means. His father came from the tribe of Ephraim and was named Elka'nah, and his mother's name was Hannah. Samuel was a child of destiny due to the covenant that his mother made with Yahweh during a period when she was old and barren.

So, it came to pass that once Samuel was born, his parents dedicated him to the Lord and placed him under the tutelage of the priest named Eli (1 Sam 1:21-28). One night this young lad was perplexed because he kept hearing a voice calling him. (1 Sam 3). Eli helped young Samuel sense a call to ministry by teaching the lad to respond properly to the voice. And once young Samuel properly responded by saying, *"Speak Lord, your servant hears,"* Samuel ultimately emerged as a judge (1 Sam 7:15-17), prophet (1 Sam 3:19-21) and priest.

As priest, Samuel was instrumental in anointing Saul as Israel's first king (1 Sam 8:4-10:1), and likewise her most celebrated king, David (1 Sam 16). Perhaps one of Samuel's weaknesses was not being able to accept King Saul's disobedience and rejection by Yahweh (1 Sam 15:10-31). Yet, his strength permeates around being faithful to the assignments that God gave him, even when they were uncomfortable for him to carry them out. We salute the life and legacy of this multi-talented servant of God as a trailblazer being the fulfillment of a praying mother. He clearly understood his role and displayed a spirit of humility throughout his life.

Saul

The saga of Saul unfolds as Israel's first king over the United Kingdom (1 Sam 9:1-31:13). A brief sequel to this detailed account is found in 1 Chronicles, Chapter 10. Saul emerged from the tribe of Benjamin and the son of Kish, who appears to be wealthy (1 Sam 9:1). In addition, Saul is introduced as an attractive and tall individual. Once anointed by Samuel, he was given the gift of prophecy (1 Sam 9:9-13) and displayed compassion and wise counsel toward the people (1 Sam 11:5-15), and it appeared that God's favor was with him. Saul was anointed to defeat the Philistines and personify a life of righteousness, but he allowed poor judgment to cause him to fall out of Yahweh's favor (1 Sam 13:8-15; 15:10-35).

Although Saul was both a sizeable man and anointed by God, he was intimidated or uncertain about how to handle the threats launched by Goliath, the Philistine giant. In addition, Saul was insecure and jealous (1 Sam 18:6-16, 29). All of these factors play out in the later part of the story, where in a desperate move to secure a victory Saul consults with the witch of Endor (1 Sam 28), and ultimately he and his sons die disgracefully in battle at the hands of their enemy, the Philistines (1 Sam 31).

We admire Saul's willingness to accept his calling as the first King of Israel, as well as his ear to hear Samuel's wise counsel. And one can argue that Saul was more stupid than rebellious, for we see a repenting heart once he was made aware of his error (1 Sam 15:24-31).

A powerful lesson is learned from the life of Saul. He is appointed king over Israel against the will of God (1 Sam 8:10-22), which is a signal for failure. Even though some of his actions were admirable, the truth is revealed in seeing his heart was not totally aligned with the will of God. Perhaps, it would have been better for him to decline the offer of king, but he could only have done so if his heart and soul was in tune with the Spirit of the Lord. We too must remember that everything offered to us is not good for us to accept.

David

Now, we come to the second most influential character in the entire Bible (after the life of Abraham). The chronicles of David is so endearing until you find them in several places in the Old Testament (1 Sam 16-31; 2 Sam 2:1-2:12 and 1 Chr 11-29). David emerged from humble beginnings being a son of Jesse in Bethlehem, and the Tribe of Judah. The call and anointing of David took place while he was a youth even though his appointment as king would not take place until many years later (1 Sam 16). And this selection takes place while Saul is king. David was adequately described in scripture (1 Sam 16:18). In other words David was a worshipper, fervently praised God and displayed tremendous courage before the Lord. He entered the service of Saul as a lad and his admirable qualities propelled him into becoming the king's armor-bearer (1 Sam 16:21). The accomplishments of David are enormous, but he too had some weaknesses. Perhaps his most famous story permeates around the poor judgment i.e. lust and pride, that resulted in taking another man's wife and ultimately marrying her and having a child (2 Sam 11). He experienced a rivalry and anarchy with his son, Absalom (2 Sam 15). David was a visionary, warrior and diplomat (1 Chr 22-29). He was given the blueprint for building a temple in Jerusalem, but God did not allow him to implement the plan. David qualities outweigh his mistakes, simply because he loved God with all his heart and soul versus the heart of Saul. Yes, *David had an affair and was a murderer*, but yet God used him and distinguished him in such a special manner until Jesus was commonly referred to as the *Son of David* (Lk 18:38). His mission was to defeat the Philistines, like his predecessor and establish a righteous kingdom (2 Sam 7). We cherish the legendary character surrounding King David because he seemed to always repent upon being made aware of his errors (2 Sam 12).

Solomon

He is referred to as the wisest and richest king of Israel. The life and legacy of Solomon can be found in 1 Kings 2-11; 1 Chr 23 through 2 Chr 9. His parents were King David and Queen Bathsheba. Solomon was a child of nobility and destined for greatness. His greatest accomplishment was to fulfill the vision of his father, David by constructing Israel's first temple (1 Chr 28:5f). Solomon was extremely wise, visionary, diplomat and was keenly aware it was God's favor that allowed him to be chosen as the third and last king of the United Kingdom (1 Kings 8). Perhaps one of his greatest weaknesses permeated around being attracted to many women and embracing idolatrous practices (1 Kings 11), thus resulting in God's disfavor and various adversaries coming against him up until his death. Solomon's strength is numerous and admirable i.e. truly loved God, consulted the wisdom of the elders and was a kingdom builder (see 2 Chronicles, Chapter 8). His notoriety is wide spread and even mentioned by Jesus Christ (Lk 12:27). We salute Solomon because he had a great taste for the finer things in life both in the temple and his palace. He knew God was the source of wisdom and righteousness, therefore, he asked for divine favor as king. He was God's anointed even though he made numerous mistakes.

Isaiah

Situated among the three major literary prophets in the Old Testament, the book of Isaiah is the longest (66 chapters) in the Old Testament. However, the memoirs of Isaiah, son of Amoz is found in Chapters 1-39. The remaining chapters reflect later periods beyond the life of Isaiah. Unlike most prophets Isaiah emerged from the ranks of nobility and his call to ministry is described in a dramatic and convincing manner (Isa 6). His mission was to declare oracles against Jerusalem & Judah and surrounding nations. In addition, he forewarned Israel of Judgment due to their idolatrous practices. He pronounced the coming of the Messianic King (Isa 9, 11) as well as gives us a glimpse into the fallen angel, Lucifer (Isa 14). Isaiah was called upon to display rather strange behavior i.e. sackcloth and ash and walk through the streets barefoot and naked for three years (Isa 20). His weakness may have been displayed in his lack of rebuke against King Hezekiah.

Ezekiel

This colorful character covers the entire book of Ezekiel (Chapters 1-48). Ezekiel is the second major literary prophet and he was born prior to the Babylonian Captivity, and this reality help shaped his theology and sociology. He was the son of a priest named Buzi, who was also taken to Babylon during the second deportation (2 Kings 24:11-16). His call to ministry is distinctly laid out in Chapter two. This catastrophic event did not alter the vision God had imparted to him for Israel. He is one of several men in the Old Testament who served as priest and prophet. Ezekiel's mission was to amplify the idolatry in Israel while at the same time speak against Babylon and the surrounding nations. He was a visionary and experienced a series of challenging messages from God. Like most prophets he too was ordered by God to display strange behaviors i.e. cutting his hair as a sign (Ezek 5), and upon the death of his wife he was ordered not to mourn (Ezek 24:15-27). Perhaps his most noted visions permeated around the *Wheel in the Middle of the Wheel* (Ezek 1:15-28), *Valley of Dry Bones* in Chapter 37, and *King of Tyre typifies Satan* (Ezek 28:1-19). We admire the resilient spirit and discipline displayed in his character. And as a result of his faithful we are able to see oracles of judgments, call to righteousness and the vision for the new temple and holy city as part of God's restoration for the righteous. If there are weaknesses of Ezekiel they are very minor.

Jeremiah

It appears he was predestined to be a prophet prior to his birth (Jer 1:4-19). The story of Jeremiah discloses another unusual character (Chapters 1-52). His father was a priest from the tribe of Benjamin. He is considered to be one of the third Major Literary Prophets in Israel. He proclaimed the message of Yahweh boldly in Israel prior to their fall in the 6th century B. C. even though he experienced disheartening sights (Jer 7-10), and faced a series of plot to kill him (Jer 11:18-23; 18:18-23). The oracles he declared caused him to be banned from Judah, imprisoned and deported to Egypt. Although he stood for righteousness all his life, yet he became disheartened and overwhelmed by the circumstances he experienced and opted to withdraw from the ministry on several occasions. Perhaps his most noted quote permeates around the quote, "If I say, I will not mention him, or speak any more in his name, there is in mine heart as it were a burning fire shut up in my bones..." (Jer 20:9). Nonetheless, his most memorable quote centers around his re-awakening moment, when he said, "His words are like fire shut up in my bones." We have learned valuable lessons from him and perhaps it can best be summed up in the allegory of the *Potter and the Clay* (Jer 18). When it was all said and done he keenly realized the message is always greater than the messenger, even though it caused him pain and discomfort in so many ways. *He was too young* (Jer 1:6) but yet God used him as a champion for righteousness.

Jonah

This is one of the Minor Prophets that unlocked the mystery behind the all-inclusive nature surrounding the call to righteousness. The story of Jonah covers Chapters 1-4, where he is identified as the son of Amittai. Here we are introduced to a man who was displeased with the assignment God gave him. More specifically God gave him a mandate to preach to one of Israel's long-standing enemy, the Assyrians in the historical city of Nineveh. His weakness can be seen in rebelling against God by going in another direction. Nonetheless, God interrupted his plans and re-directed him to go there, despite his personal opinion (Chapter 1). His rebellion could have caused his life but we see the mercies of God displayed in Chapter 2. Once he was aware it is God's way or no other way, he obeys and made the trip to Nineveh in less time than usual. Upon entering the city he proclaimed a message of repentance, wherein the people adhered. Nonetheless this pleased God but ended up displeasing Jonah (Chapter 4) and God had to remind him through an allegory. Jonah seemed to be a moody and prejudice individual steeped in his cultural and history more so than the liberating power of the Most High God. The history of Nineveh in relation to Israel was clear but the saving grace of God is far greater. *Jonah ran from God* (Jonah 1:3) but yet God used him. We salute Jonah for finally obeying the voice of God by transcending his comfort zone and delivering a message to a foreign people despite his personal feelings.

Job

The story of Job is both mystical and revealing when it comes to getting a handle on why does the righteous suffer? The recounting of his faith and relationship with God is seen in Chapters 1-42. The story is legendary and there are some who contend he was a fictitious character, however, I firmly disagree with this assumption. He has no ancestral references (similar to Elijah) but comes from the land of Uz. Some historians believe it is the same as Edom. The name Job means hostile or penitent. It appears Job was a priest and very honorable man. In addition, he was very wealthy. The character of Job was so impressive until Satan requested from God to allow him to afflict his body and family (Chapter 1). Strangely we see God complies with the request because He had confidence in Job. Subsequently Job lost his 10 children, servants, property, respect in the community and the confidence of his wife. His friends heard about his misfortune, came to his house, and sat for days, falsely accusing him. His call permeated around suffering and living righteously in the midst of false accusations. When you study the story of Job it appears there are two distinct characters. He definitely display doubt, frustration and discouragement, while at the same time he displays strength i.e. Job 35:9. His weaknesses can be seen throughout the scriptures. For example, Job 3:1-19 and Job 14. Perhaps these verses help us understand Job's dilemma i.e. "Oh, that I knew where I might find him...Behold I go forward and he is not there; and backward, but I cannot perceive him..." Job 23:2-17. In the end Job teaches us a profound lesson in forgiveness (Chapter 42), and in so doing God gave him more than he had previously. Remember, *Job went bankrupt,* but yet God used him.

Mary

The story of Mary, the Mother of Jesus is quite interesting. Both Matthew and Luke recount the selection of Mary being chosen to become the Mother of Jesus and the birth of the Savior (Mt 1-2; Lk 1-3). According to the scriptures she is traced through King David's lineage (Mt 1:1-17) all the way back to Abraham. She appears to be a typical

Hebrew girl who found herself impregnated by the Holy Spirit with the Messiah (Mt 1:20). This obviously caused embarrassment to her due to being engaged to Joseph. Both Matthew and Luke give commentary on the way Joseph accepted this reality. Her mission was to give birth and nurture the Savior of the World. Once again, I do not see any weakness or resistance in this female carrying out her mandate. She is admired for realizing who her son really was and followed his teachings (Jn 2:1-12). We salute her because even in death she remained a faithful follower of her son even to the death of the cross (Jn 19:25-27).

John the Baptist

He is by far one of the most colorful and boldest prophets since the prophet Elijah. The longest narrative giving an overview of his life and demeanor is found in Matthew, Chapter 3. He was a cousin of Jesus and the son of Elizabeth and Zachariah. His parents were elderly but faithful to the covenant (Lk Chapter 1). Their story reminds us of Abraham and Sarah. However, please review the other scriptures describing his activities (Jn 3:22-4:1; Lk 3:15-20; Mk 1:12-15, 3:18-22). His name is revered throughout Hebraic tradition, and this was clearly seen during a conversation with Jesus and his disciples (Mt 16:14). His mission was to serve as a trail-blazer or fore-runner for the Messiah. His behavior and lifestyle were strange i.e. wore camel's hair, leather girdle and ate locusts and honey. He was summoned by God to deliver a stern message of righteousness to the religious and political leaders (Mt 3:7-10). This spiritual mandate caused him to be incarcerated and beheaded. I do not see any rebellion in his character or calling. His resilient spirit and faithfulness to God is admirable. He was simple, righteous and fearless. His ministry was relatively short but effective and memorable.

Peter

The Apostle Peter is by far the most out spoken and most recognized disciple of Jesus Christ. His life and legacy is found in all four Gospels. In addition, there are two books (1 Peter and 2 Peter) accredited to his authorship. I have written another book, *Discipleship (7 Lessons)* addressing the character of each disciple. The call of Peter is documented in the following Gospels (Mt 5:18-23; Mk 1:16-20; Lk 5:1-11; and Jn 1:35-42). He was a professional fisherman and a married man (Mk 1:29-31). Nonetheless, he abandoned that career and embraced Jesus as the Messiah. He is the first disciple to publicly recognize him as the Messiah (Mt 16:13-20). The name Peter in the Greek is *Petros* and Aramaic is *Kepha or Ceohas*. These names denote rock/faith or a man of courage. He seemed to be the first to speak even if it was incorrect. For example, Peter saw Jesus walking upon the sea and impulsively asked permission to join him (Mt 14:28). Whenever the disciples are listed Peter's name is always listed first (Mt 10:2). He was called to lead the disciples along with boldly proclaiming the Gospel of the Kingdom. His most noticeable weakness centered upon denying the one whom he loved so dearly during the passion week of Jesus (Lk 22:47-62). He was rebuked by Jesus repeatedly (Jn 13; Lk 22:50-52). Despite his flaws who would not love to have someone like Peter as part of their ministry. He loved God wholeheartedly and you never had to wonder what was on his mind.

James

He was one of the disciples in the inner circle of Jesus. The recounting of the call of James, the son of Zeb-e-dee is found in Mark 1:19-20. James, like Peter was a fisherman. In addition, to various gospel references the Epistle of James is accredited to the Apostle James. He was also referred to as the brother of John. James and John's mother was very ambitious and wanted the best for her sons. For example, on one occasion she asked Jesus if they could sit on the right and left side when he reigns in His kingdom (Mt 20:20-28; Mk 10:35-45). It appears that James placed a lot of emphasis on the importance of working alongside faith. Jesus saw great potentials in him, and that is why he was considered to be in the inner circle during Jesus' final days (Mt 26:36-46; Mk 14:32-42; Lk 22:40-46). Perhaps James' weaknesses were displayed in the aforementioned examples of going along with his mother's request for power and prestige, and failure to show resilience in prayer during Jesus final hour. Nonetheless we can salute him for his the theological treatise or sermon displayed in the Epistle of James, as well as his being a martyr of the Church (Acts 12:2).

John

He was the brother of James and son of Zebedee. It appears they lived in Galilee, a fisherman's haven. The call of John took place at the same time as his brother James. He is commonly called the beloved disciple (Jn 19:26-27). Traditionally the following books are accredited to his authorship: John, 1 John, 2 John, 3 John and Revelation. John seemed to have understood the motivational principle of God, which is love. All the writings accredited to John seems to have keen insight into the son-ship and Lordship of Jesus Christ (Jn 20:30-31). Martin Luther, the German Reformation theologian said the gospel in miniature is expressed in John 3:16. John read, circled, and he accompanied Peter to see the tomb where Christ previously laid (Jn 21). Upon reading the gospels you get a sense of gratitude and compassion being articulated by John. His weaknesses are basically the same as his brother. Nonetheless, we salute him for the outstanding example of faith and love.

Judas

The story surrounding the call Judas is found in Luke 6:12-19 and Mark 3:13-19. Due to the flaw in his character Judas is always listed last among the disciples. He is referred to as the *Son of Perdition* (Jn 17:12) or the most memorable act centered upon the betrayal of Jesus (Mt 26:47-56; Mk 14:43-52; Lk 22:47-53; Jn 18:1-11). Despite the spirit of greed and betrayal of Judas we must never lose sight of the fact that Jesus saw something in him worthy enough to select him as a disciple. Early in Jesus ministry we got a glimpse of Judas character when Mary used expensive ointment on Jesus feet (Jn 12:2-8). Nonetheless, we should remember the name Judas is a derivative of Judah, the fourth son of Jacob. The name Judah basically means praise and perhaps this is why Satan targeted him to betray Jesus. In the final analysis there seemed to be remorse on his part for the sin he committed (Mt 27:3-10), even though it did not alter the sacrifice Christ must make on the cross. Therefore, Judas remains a mysterious Biblical character because he definitely was called. However he allowed the seed of unrighteousness to cultivate in his heart, thereby nullifying and voiding his righteous calling.

Phillip

The story of Phillip is relatively short and is found in Acts of the Apostles Chapters 6:1-8 and 8:26-40. There seems to be no ancestral references; however, it appears he was a faithful member of the Body of Christ assembled in Jerusalem subsequent to the Day of Pentecost. He was appointed to serve as a Deacon due to a dispute between the Hebrews and Grecian women. Aside from this appointment it appears he was also divinely called when a need arose surrounding the Ethiopian Eunuch's lack of understanding the scriptures (Acts 8:26-40). I do not see any weaknesses in his character. He was bold and obedient when the spirit directed him. He is mentioned later in Paul's career (Acts 21:7-14) wherein Paul describes him as an evangelist. This character clearly demonstrates a lay member being called to serve as an evangelist.

Apollos

The story surrounding the life and ministry of Apollos clearly demonstrate he was a man with exceptional talents and charisma (Acts 18:24-28). According to the aforementioned scriptures he was born in Alexandria, Egypt. His zeal and insights into the scriptures caused many to believe on the Lord Jesus Christ. Apollos clearly demonstrates each of us must utilize our skills to the best of their abilities and must remain open-minded to heighten our awareness concerning greater revelations (Acts Chapter 19). His name is also mentioned by Paul in Titus 3:13 as a traveling companion. He helped organize the Church at Corinth (1 Cor 3:1-9). Apollos further reminds us there is room for intellectuals and eloquent speakers in the Church as long as we remain humble before the Lord.

Dorcas

The story of Dorcas, surnamed Tabitha is relatively short (Acts 9:36-41). It appears she lived in the seaport city called Joppa, which was the same place Jonah launched from in an attempt to flee from his assignment. Dorcas was a humble servant of God who delighted in sharing in *Alms deeds* or charitable works. More specifically she was known to sew and give to the poor. Upon her passing the word got to Peter in a neighboring city and requested him to come to their aid. Upon arriving Peter followed the example of Jesus and prayed for her restoration. She was raised from the dead and this caused many to believe in the Lord. Once again it appears the women in ministry did not display any rebellion or disobedience with their spiritual mandate. We salute her quiet and persistent way of carrying out the mission of the Church. It is very clear she understood the spiritual authority inherent in serving (Lk 4:18; Rom 12:13, 28; Gal 6:10). Remember the road to greatness is grounded in humility and servant hood.

Timothy

The story and ministry of Timothy reflects a young man who had been brought up in the Church (2 Tim 3:14-15) but lacked the theological training and spiritual maturity until he met the Apostle Paul. The First and Second Epistles are accredited to Timothy. He is also introduced in Acts 16:3 as a new companion of Paul due to a disagreement between Paul and Barnabas. The name Timothy means *Honored by God.* His father was Greek and his mother a Hebrew, thus making him what we call a *mixed child* and that in itself caused unique challenges during that era. Timothy was a faithful servant of God and mentee of Paul. In both Epistles there seem to be an emphasis on embracing sound Church doctrines and avoiding false teaching and heresies. He gives us insights into effective worship, role of women in ministry, Deacons, Bishops, treatment of widows and elders. He was fearless and understood his calling as an Evangelist, Pastor and Teacher. What I like most about Timothy is his loyalty and respect for his mentor, Paul. And the reason his writings are so seasoned is because he had a great example before him. There is truth in the axiom that says, *"The fruit does not fall far from the tree."*

Barnabas

He too was a traveling companion of the Apostle Paul. Barnabas was introduced in scripture as part of the Jerusalem Church. His initial assignment was to go before Antioch and bring Paul to the Jerusalem Council. (Acts 11:22-30). Within these verses we get a clear picture of his character i.e. good man, full of the Holy Spirit and of faith. He was a faithful witness and this resulted in many souls being saved. Perhaps the most noticeable moment in his illustrious ministerial career permeated around the separation between Paul and Barnabas as a result of what to do with the novice, John Mark (Acts 15:36-41). It appears there are no flaws or sense of rebellion in his character. We salute his maturity, boldness and soul-winning spirit during the *Early Church.*

Silas

This Biblical character is introduced in Acts of the Apostles as another one of Paul's missionary companion after the parting of the way with Barnabas (Acts 15:41). He traveled extensively with Paul and his zeal and passion for the gospel is displayed in Acts Chapter 16. While in Philippi, both he and Paul were attacked and jailed. They prayed and God miraculously released them at midnight. Both he and Timothy separated from Paul in Berea (Acts 17:14-15). All in all there appears to be thirteen New Testament references of Silas. He was loyal and faithful to Paul and the ministry. His calling seemed to permeate around being both an evangelist and prophet (Acts 15:32). There seemed to be no rebellious or disobedient spirit observed in his character. Therefore, we salute him as an example noteworthy of studying and emulating.

Ananias & Sapphira

This is the only illustration of Biblical characters wherein I will disclose information surrounding a couple. The story surrounding this couple is relatively short but it has left a profound lesson regarding dishonesty in the Church (Acts 5:1-11). During the Early Church, not only were there evidence of the Pentecostal outpouring, but there were also genuine acts of kindness and fellowship (Acts 2:43-47; 3:32-37) which clearly reminds us about the mission of the Church. The story of Ananias and Sapphira deviates from that paradigm, by withholding part of the revenue for personal gain. Apparently, others were selling properties and bringing all the profits to the Apostles in order for them to disburse according to the saints in need. Peter was able to discern what they were doing and confronted about it. Obviously they both agreed on the lie and as a result they died separately in the course of the same day. Apparently they were prominent and respectable members of the Jerusalem Church but their willingness to be influenced by Satan caused them to experience an untimely death. This swift hand of judgment served as a wake-up call for the Body of Christ. Thus far Sapphira is the only female who displayed a disobedient spirit. All of us must learn from this negative example and be truthful, especially when the Lord allows us to experience profit from the sale of property or otherwise.

Paul

The Apostle Paul is perhaps the most influential character in the New Testament other than Jesus Christ. The saga of Saul, who later became known as Paul can be found in Acts Chapters 9-28. In addition, there are thirteen epistles (Romans, 1 Corinthians, 2 Corinthians, Galatians, Ephesians, Philippians, Colossians, 1 Thessalonians, 2 Thessalonians, 1 Timothy, 2 Timothy, Titus, Philemon) written by him. During Paul's arrest and defense of the gospel he gives us a sense of where he came from and the things he did prior to his conversion (Acts 22:3-5). After Paul's conversion, he becomes a champion for Christ. He boldly defended the faith and launched three missionary journeys throughout Europe and Asia Minor. He felt his calling and mission was to be an *Apostle to the Gentiles* (Rom 11:13; 15:16), even though there were those who questioned his Apostolic authority (1 Cor 9:1). He was a prolific writer and possessed exceptional rhetorical skills. He had both Roman and Jewish citizenship, thus enabling him to navigate effectively throughout the Greco-Roman world. I have another publication entitled; *Doctrines of the Church*, which to a large degree are concepts developed by the Apostle Paul where he articulated them more so than anyone else. The doctrines are as followed: God (Theology); Jesus Christ (Christology); Angels (Angelology); Demons (Demonology); Man (Anthropology); Sin (Harmartiology); Salvation (Soteriology); Church (Ecclesiology); Last Days (Eschatology). Although he was gifted in the five-fold Administrative Gifts, Paul was a practical man, and utilized his skills as a tentmaker to sustain himself and help others (Acts 18:3). Paul was obedient to his gifts and calling, and detected no rebellion or disobedience in his character. However, he was not the one to back down from a challenge or accusation. For example, the twelfth chapter of Second Corinthians recounts Paul boasting due to a series of false allegations. Furthermore, he seemed to have been bothered by a lingering condition in his body. When it was all said and done Paul keenly realized the purpose and mission of Grace, "My grace is sufficient for you, for my power is made perfect in weakness. I will all the more gladly boast of my weaknesses, that the power of Christ may rest upon me. For the sake of Christ, then, I am content with weaknesses, insults, hardships, persecution, and calamities; for when I am weak I am strong." (2 Cor 12:9-10). Tradition has it that he died in Rome as a martyr. Perhaps, the best way to sum up his illustrious ministerial career is let him speak for himself. "For I am already on the point of being sacrificed; the time of my departure has come. I have fought a good fight, I have finished the race, and I have kept the faith. Henceforth there is laid up for me the, the crown of righteousness, which the Lord, the righteous judge, will reward me on that Day, and not only me but all who have loved his appearing." Of course, we can go on and on about this controversial yet faithful witness. The nature and destiny of the Church is better understood because of his significant contribution. Remember, *Paul was too religious and a persecutor of the Church*, but God used him mightily.

Jesus Christ

There is not enough time and space to adequately describe or articulate His contribution, and the impact He made at the turn of the first century B.C. In order to grasp the dynamism and animation radiating through Him perhaps all four Gospels could be a good launching point. Matthew, Mark and Luke are referred to as Synoptic Gospels, due to their literary narrative disclosure of the Life and Teachings of Jesus. Matthew and Luke give us back ground into his ancestry in the opening chapters. Mark deviates from that pattern by declaring Jesus clearly ushered in the message of the *Kingdom of God* (Mk 1:14-15). Alternatively, John focused on the humanity (Son of Man) and divinity (Son of God) and the eternal purpose of His coming. By and large the Old Testament gives a forecast of the coming Messiah i.e. Isaiah Chapters 7 and 9. While the New Testament actually embraces him in the Gospels, and Acts of the Apostles and the Epistles point back to his ministry. Jesus is uniquely identified as the *Seed of Abraham* (Lk 1:55; Gal 3:29; Heb 2:16) and the *Son of David* (Mk 10:47-48; 12:35; Mt 15:22). Jesus is definitely an historical figure but we reverence Him as the anointed one. The kingdom established by Jesus is identified with three unique personalities i.e. Priest, Prophet and King. I have another publication entitled, *Kingdom of God (12 Lessons)* detailing their distinct roles. He is both mystery and truth. His glorious return will usher in a series of judgments on the earth and the annihilation of Satan and all the evil in this world. He has established the Church within the Dispensation of Grace, wherein she serves as his official representative on earth (Mt 16:18). In addition, He has disbursed the Gift of the Holy Spirit to govern and empower the saints (Acts 2) within the global community. He was obedient to His Father even in the face of death. He had no flaws (1 Pet 2:22) but yet He was humiliated and died for the sins of the world. During his final agonizing moment his humanity spoke out, "My God, my God, why hast thou forsaken me?" (Mt 17:46). However, I do not consider this a flaw but rather the human frailty being expressed. His exemplary life enables us to be reconciled with the Father. He rose from obscurity in Nazareth (Jn 1:46) to shame and prominence in Jerusalem. And even death and the grave was not able to defeat Him (1 Cor 15:55-57). The titles and phrases associated with Him are quite impressive and encouraging i.e. *King of Kings, Lord of Lord, Prince of Peace,*

51

Wonderful, Faithful, Amen, Lily of the Valley, Rose of Sharon, conquering Savior Lion and Tribe of Judah, Burden Bearer, Good Shepherd, Lamb of God and I Am etc.

Notes

Chapter 7
Practical Guidelines and Virtues for Effective Ministry

1. **A Life of Holiness**—The Bible serves as our spiritual roadmap and enables us to navigate through this temporal and sensuous world. If you study the scriptures you will come to realize that the nature or essence of God is holy. And holiness is not an abstract term, but rather a prescribed way of life. Therefore, you cannot be serious about worship and service unless we understand and embrace holiness. The Hebrew term *Qadas* denotes being set apart or separated for a sacred use. The profane and carnal nature cannot dwell in your spirit if you are going to be effective with your gifts and calling. It is imperative that we be keenly aware of God's holy presence at all times. This awareness is something like being on your best behavior when your mother is around. Please do not allow religion, traditions, rituals, or anything else to persuade you to bring reproach or abomination to the church or yourself while you are claiming to be a servant of the Most High God.

2. **Humility**—This virtue is at the core of Jesus' unique, persuasive and liberating message surrounding the Gospel of the Kingdom of God. True power is grounded in humility and not arrogance. For example, everyone will readily attest that the lion is king of the jungle. However, the elephant, rhino and hippo are much stronger, but they chose not to make all the fuss like the lion. This further reminds me of an Ashanti Proverb from Ghana. It says, "The hen knows when it is day break, but she allows the rooster to make the announcement." The Hebrew term *Kana & Sapel* refers to sinking down, being subdued and void of pride or self-exaltation or to bring low. Both the minister and layperson must always be mindful that they are Ambassadors or representatives of Christ.

3. **Patience**—This virtue is a very valuable enabling tool in the life of a minister or laity an illustration of this can be seen in the life of King David. Samuel anointed him to become king years before he was actually appointed. Patience is a methodical and delayed method of teaching and developing godly character. Everything operates according to times and seasons. I recall the insightful words of Dr. George M. James in his book, *Stolen Legacy*. He said, "Nature does nothing in vain, but according to definite and prescribe laws. She is always working from the less perfect to the more perfect." Knowing when to speak and

function on behalf of God to the group cannot be done prematurely. Learn to listen, observe, submit and be quiet, because they will compliment the spirit of patience.

4. **Effective Communication**—Two of my mentors, Dr. Arenia C. Mallory and Dr. Isaac Clark left lasting impressions on me, simply because they constantly challenged and encouraged me to develop my writing and oral skills. As a rule of thumb, I will write my sermons, because sermons must be viewed as spiritual masterpieces. I have written a booklet entitled, *Introduction to Homiletics* and it explores the art of sermonizing through creative channels of communication. There is nothing more frustrating than trying to express a thought or an idea to an audience that is uninterested because they cannot understand your presentation. There is very little tolerance for persons who opt to be ignorant and fail to invest in the development of their dialoging skills. Rehearse by yourself and then before a family member or friend, knowing that your final audience will better receives your message once you build your confidence and hone your delivery skills. In addition, you must overcome the spirit of inertia or laziness, commonly observed in the faith community, due to failing to study and write. Once you discover the joy of writing you will be the first to observe if your thoughts have been conveyed in a thoughtful and convincing manner prior to sharing it with others. Putting it another way, the people of Khamit (Egypt) initiated writing thousands of years ago and we are yet marveling and studying their gift to humanity. Therefore, you must begin to recognize and appreciate that your writings will not be restricted to your lifetime.

5. **Devotion**—Throughout my developmental years, God blessed me by placing righteous and spiritual role models before me who not only advised me about what was really important in life, but also lived demonstrative lifestyles. Because my parents used to have the whole family gather for 6:00 a.m. prayer, every weekday prior to my leaving for school, I developed a strong *prayer life* as a child. Then while I was attending the Church of God in Christ boarding school, Saints Academy and Junior College, (Lexington, MS) President Dr. Mallory likewise mandated that all dormitory students participate in 6:00 a.m. prayer in their dormitories prior to leaving for breakfast or attending classes. Consequently, I have led prayer since June 1989 at the Church where I serve as Pastor in Milwaukee, Wisconsin, every Monday through Friday. Prayer is a spiritual

enabling tool that allows the believer to petition God about an array of concerns, so that He might make a judgment or ruling based upon what is best for us. Prayer is a vehicle that transports us spiritually into the presence of the Almighty while at the same time teaches us how to remain patient and grow in faith. Being intellectual and anointed can produce rewarding experiences, but nothing takes the place of praying. Take time to pray personally and corporately, so that you will began to gain a true sense of belonging within the Kingdom of God. There is no substitute or excuse when it comes to praying.

The next ingredient pertaining to devotion permeates around *fasting*. The discipline of fasting has to do with abstinence or denying oneself from food and or water. I vividly recall my parents going on a three-day fast or consecration while at the same time maintaining their regular duties along with attending worship several times a week. On a weekly basis our household fasts two to three days per week. Respectively, we have undergone fasting from five to forty days. There is no way you can deny yourself physically and spiritually without ultimately becoming sensitive to the mind and purpose of God. Fasting may disfigure you physically speaking but internally you will gain strength and a resolution to reach new horizons.

Earlier I touched upon the value of **studying**. However, I want to emphasize the importance of applying yourself to accessing knowledge and understanding about both the sacred and secular world we live in. In 1997, I led a group of 74 African-American youths and adults from Milwaukee and Oklahoma City to Senegal, Gambia and Ghana under the flagship program entitled, *Operation Return*. Prior to taking this pilgrimage the youth had to study the culture, geography, trade and commerce, government, and language of each country we visited. Studying is a unique way of informing and empowering an individual even if they live in impoverished conditions. "No man can be a slave unless he releases his will to a master." The book of Proverbs is an excellent source to inspire you while at the same time introduces you to the path of wisdom. Your gift and calling can easily become dormant if you fail to study the Bible and other resourceful materials.

The discipline of **praising** is also critical, but in my opinion Satan has masterfully bombarded us with so many troubles and challenges that we often find ourselves failing to praise tp God anyhow. Praise is grounded in rejoicing and being vibrant in our

56

spirit in the midst of good and bad times. Praising God has a mystical way of propelling you through the storms of life and allowing you to see the glory and majesty of God. There is victory in the praise of the righteous. "Painful experiences will lead toward growth, and not pleasant ones." (De Mello). I admonish you to read passages from the Psalms every day because they will teach you how to praise and worship God.

By and large the Body of Christ has been steered away from the discipline of *meditation*, which is our last ingredient within the area of devotion. However, Saints of God must learn to embrace quiet, tranquil and peaceful environments in order to go deeper into the mind of God. We were created and called to live peacefully; however, sin and evil are here to disrupt this tranquil state of being. Yet, we can conquer this disruption, by employing each of the above devotional ingredients, all so that we might have a more enriched experience with God and develop an over-coming spirit in this present world.

6. **Willingness to Serve**—There must be a willing and obedient spirit when it comes to working in the ministry. *Serving* can be very challenging because of the diverse personalities you will come in contact with. The Apostle Paul gives several great analogies regarding servant hood. For example, he mentioned that the *Farmer, Athlete and Soldier* have unique and distinct roles in society. The farmer who plants early and cultivates is expected to receive a great harvest. The athlete who conditions and competes according to the rules is expected to win. And the soldier does not function like a civilian, but rather complies with orders and directives given to him. In order to serve, you must rid yourself of selfishness and personal agendas. In addition, you must be willing to work on behalf of the greater good and view yourself as a team player.

7. **Faithfulness to the ministry and your assignment**—The success of your mission in ministry on earth hinges to a large degree on how faithful you are. The aforementioned illustration i.e. farmer, athlete and soldier must display faithfulness to their assignments if they expect a favorable result. The same word in Hebrew for faith (Aman) is closely related to the word we use in closing prayer *Amen*. To say Amen is to say so be it or it is so. In both cases they denote certainty, stability, resilient, ferocity, and endurance. In addition, the term *faith* is the same word for rock. There is no need to have faith unless you are willing to be challenged and tested. All of our experiences come to make us

better, not bitter. Being faithful to the ministry requires steadfastness of purpose. St. Augustine once said, "Faith is to believe in that which we cannot see, and the reward of faith is to see that which we believe." Do not abort your assignment or become slack in your responsibilities due to adversities. Instead, take both the negative and positive experiences and use them as building blocks in your most holy faith. The four elements: earth, air, fire, and water are faithful. The conditions of these elements—hot, cold, wet, and dry—are also examples of faithfulness. The animal, vegetation and mineral kingdoms are faithful to their callings in nature. However, the greatest challenge lies within the spiritual kingdom of man and woman. I can still hear the resounding words of my high school principal and mentor, Mr. Joseph Davis saying, "Do right because it is right to do right."

Notes

Chapter 8

Contemporary Ecclesiastical Structures

In this section, I want you to keep in mind that there is creativity and diversity in the Body of Christ. Some Churches adhere to episcopacy while others embrace a congregational order. Simply stated, the Episcopal congregations have Bishops at the hierarchy of their ecclesiastical structure. Alternatively, a congregational orientated body will have an Ordained Minister who is appointed or elected, but who is not referred to as a Bishop.

All religious entities within the Church recognize some form of ordination. Such ordination is merely the public acknowledgment, and the anointing by laying on of hands upon an individual by the Church's hierarchy. Thus the ordained minister becomes duly authorized to represent that religious entity in a variety of ecclesiastical offices i.e. pastor, evangelist, teacher, prophet, and etc. In addition, ordained clergy are duly authorized to officiate weddings, dedications, funerals, counseling, baptismal, anniversaries and at a variety of public and private settings.

Even further, ordained ministers must reflect maturity because they not only represent their organization but the Body of Christ at large. Prior to ordination the individual who senses a divine calling will usually undergo a period of training, during which he or she is recognized as a novice or minister.

Yet, the diversity within the Church is so vast until it has created deep concerns for me and for those who truly love Christ. While there is no debate within her ranks about Jesus Christ being Lord and Savior, it is prudent that I share a few practical illustrations about how doctrinal, ecclesiastical, denominational and practical realities have created unique challenges for us.

Within Christendom, there are two major classifications or fractions called *Catholicism and Protestantism*. The history of the Catholic Church is linked to the Apostle Peter's Confession, Apostolic confession, the Vatican or Rome and the Nicene Council. At the helm of this body there is the Papacy or Pope, who is commonly referred to as the Holy Father. Surrounding him are seasoned men, called Cardinals or Archbishops, who have come through the ranks of the Bishopric.

In addition, there are Bishops, Priests or Fathers and Ordained Deacons. The Catholic Church is the only Christian entity that has official diplomatic status in the United Nation, due to the Vatican being recognized as a Holy and Sovereign Nation.

Martin Luther, a German theologian who became disgruntled with the doctrine and lifestyle of the Catholic Church, spearheaded the Protestant Reformation. He was inspired to withdraw and give a series of theological insights on the dispensation of grace. Part of this contention rested upon the assertion that the Pope should not have exclusive rights to interpreting the scripture.

Within the framework of Protestantism here are a few examples of religious entities commonly identified as denominations: Church of God in Christ, National Baptist Convention, National Baptist Convention USA, Progressive Baptist, Full Gospel Baptist, African Methodist Episcopal, Christian Methodist Episcopal, United Methodist, United Presbyterian, Unitarian, United Church of Christ, Full Gospel, Non-Denominational, Word Church, Apostolic, Pentecostal Assemblies of the World, Fire Baptized, Four Square, Church of the Latter Day Saints (Mormons), Seven Day Adventist, Jehovah Witnesses, and Least of These International Ministries etc.

By no means have I exhausted the list, because literally speaking there are thousands of groups, and new ones emerge every day. The members of the body are diverse, and new terminologies and phrases keep popping up. For example, there are those who refer to themselves as Pentecostal Holiness, Charismatic, and Full Gospel, Jesus Only, Word Church, Evangelical, and Apostolic.

The clergies may be referred by a variety of names, such as, Bishop, Apostle, Overseer, Reverend, Elder, Missionary, Prophet, Chaplain, Evangelist, etc. The traditions and cultures within these religious entities are diverse, and it is best to be informed and respectful when you fellowship with various ministries.

Some of the greatest debates and challenges we face have to do with the interpretation of scriptures. In all cases the founders and leaders of these groups felt an urgency to pull away from an existing religious body and usher in a new and fresh interpretation of scripture or approach to ministry. Doctrinally speaking, it is ridiculous to observe the spirit of division and some of the attitudes commonly displayed, even though they all claim to be under the banner of the Church.

Listed below are just a few examples of controversial issues that continue to cause concern and quite often alienate us from each other: The formula used for water baptism i.e. whether to baptize in Jesus' name or in the name of the Father, Son and Holy Ghost. In some religious circles women are not recognized as persons called to ministry, and they are not ordained. And there is much debate concerning the role and operation of the Holy Spirit in the Church, such as, is it relevant to speak in unknown tongues? Are the elements used for Holy Communion the actual body of Christ or symbolic? Are Heaven and Hell actual places prepared for the saints and sinners? What is the role of the Church in the Last Days? What is the Kingdom of God? What is the mission of the Church? How should homosexuality be viewed in the life of the Church? How should we view adultery? Why does the Church remain racially divided? How do you define denomination? Why is there evil in a world that claims to be full of the goodness of God?

These and countless other questions have divided us more than they have united us. Therefore, in my personal opinion, I see religion and personalities causing serious problems within the Church. Traditions, doctrines, dress codes, creeds, codes of ethics, ceremonies, and rituals definitely have their places in ministry, because the Church has the unique ability to be creative and innovative. However, we must safeguard the spirit of humility and servant hood that we clearly saw in the life and teachings of Jesus Christ.

Notes

Chapter 9

Church and Society (The Great Commission)

Everything in life is guided by principles and mandates. The Bible serves as the official manual or roadmap for the Church. However, these principles are usually carried out through persons elected or appointed to leadership roles, and whenever we add the human dimension to this spiritual equation therein opens the door to potential flaws and disappointments.

In a similar manner Jesus Christ established the Church on earth (not in heaven) in order to make her a replica of what is actually in heaven. For example, the Lord's Prayer serves as a vivid reminder of spiritual and delegated authority wherein Jesus came to establish the Kingdom of God on this earth (Mt 6:9-13; Lk 11:2-4). In addition, Jesus, The Anointed One laid out the mission of the Church when he publicly launched His ministry in a Synagogue filled with religious leaders (Lk 4:16-23) who were misrepresenting the truth.

The Church represents the liberating and delivering presence of a holy and loving God. However, the concrete realities, such as poverty, mis-education, violence, diseases, racism, corruption, wars and exploitation etc. confronting us permeate around value systems and personalities that may not necessarily align themselves spiritually with the message of the Kingdom. The Kingdom of God is spiritual in nature and is the sphere where God is sovereign.

I like to view the Church being full of Ambassadors for Christ. Generally speaking, an Ambassador is the highest ranking diplomat representing their government with a delegation in another country. We should always keep in mind that the Ambassador has the full backing and undergirding support of his or her nation as long as they serve faithfully. The values and principles of this kingdom cannot be compromised. We must be girded in righteousness and always carry the flame of evangelism (Mt 28:18-20). While representing the Church as Ambassadors we must be abreast of the diverse forms of governments in this world (see my publication, *The Kingdom of God: 12 Lessons*).

The Apostle Paul gives us several scenarios of the Church functioning in a secular world by presenting her as a Temple, Bride and Family. Nonetheless, we must understand the penetrating and dynamic spirit inherent in her mission. We must respect and adhere to the various branches of government in the USA, i.e. Legislative, Judicial and Executive. Moreover, this system of checks and balances is carried out at every level of government, i.e. federal, state, and county, city, villages and townships.

The United States government and governments throughout the world have diverse, primitive and impressive forms of governments. In addition, we are called upon to spread the Gospel of the Kingdom to various cultures and ethnic groups around the world. We must be very careful and learn from the lessons of Christian History around the world where missionaries have mis-represented Christ by imposed a racist and self-righteous spirit upon various cultures. Case in point would be missionaries worked alongside colonial rulers from Europe and America during the grueling nightmare of American Chattel Slavery. When it was all said and done Africa was colonized, resources were taken, lifestyles were disrupted and the gospel of the Kingdom of God was distorted. Despite the good and evil reality displayed in all societies we are reminded that all of these environments are temporal, while the Kingdom of God is eternal.

The Church has a mandate to seize the opportunity to serve in a godly manner at all times (Gal 6:10). In addition, members of the faith community must broaden their perspective and willingly serve as elected or appointed officials within our communities (Prov 29:2), because the righteous will make a difference. Based upon the history of this nation and the ruthless atrocities launched against African Americans, it is somewhat refreshing to see who ultimately controls history.

On November 4, 2008 God allowed Senator Barack Obama, an African American to become the forty-fourth President of the United States of America.

The psyche of racism and all the other divisive things in this country remain in tact, but the election serves as a vivid reminder, "No lie can live forever." On Labor Day 2008, I attended a rally in Milwaukee where he was the keynote speaker. Obama is gifted, full of charisma and has a passion to serve. A unique mantle of leadership has been passed on to him during a critical juncture in world history. I have no doubt he is anointed to help heal the racial, economical, political, educational, educational, psychological, social, and spiritual barriers in this nation. His life serves as a prime contemporary example of someone being called and gifted, even though he may not fit the conventional definition. His vision is clear and his passion for change is amazing.

In essence, I have simply tried to show that the gospel does not float in *La-La Land,* but rather she operates and permeates through challenging and embarrassing realities in order to bring the best out of a bad situation. Gifts and callings are designed to bring glory to Christ. And God selects and ignites individuals to serve where He deems it necessary and appropriate at unique epochs in history. "Righteousness exalts a nation, but sin is a reproach to any people." (Prov 14:34)

Notes

Chapter 10

Review and Questions

1. What is a gift?
2. What fascinates you most about the origin and purpose of gifts?
3. Define Spiritual Gifts according to the scriptures?
4. List and describe the Administrative Gifts.
5. List and describe five additional Spiritual Gifts.
6. What is a divine calling?
7. Make the distinction between gifts and callings.
8. Select and comment on five of the biblical characters.
9. Name and describe the couple who rebelled and met untimely deaths.
10. Describe the character of the disciple named Judas.
11. What is the anointing?
12. Who was anointed even though he was not in the covenant community?
13. Define and comment on the three personalities associated with the anointing.
14. Typically what public display is carried out when someone is anointed?
15. What is the role of the Holy Spirit within the Church?
16. When listing the Administrative Gifts, which offices always come first and second?
17. Name the categories of Spiritual Gifts, and which one impresses you the most?
18. How would you describe Moses?
19. Name the three most important Biblical characters, and why is this so?
20. How would you describe Job?
21. Why is Paul's contribution so important to the Church?
22. Describe the mystery and truth surrounding Jesus Christ.
23. What is holiness?
24. How important is devotion to a person with a gift and calling?
25. What is the nature of God?
26. What motivates God to work on our behalf?
27. What should be the demeanor of a follower of Christ?
28. What does it means to be ordained?
29. What does it mean to be an Episcopal church?
30. What does it mean to be a congregational church?
31. How do we describe the Protestant and Catholic Churches?

32. List some of the issues that cause alienation in the Church?
33. What is the mission of the Church?
34. Who is Christ?
35. What and where is the Kingdom of God?
36. Do you recognize your gift or calling, if so please describe?
37. Please mail or email me a 3-5 page summary of your gift and calling. Thanks. stampleyministries@gmail.com.

Chapter 11

Summary

My mission in writing is to shed some light on the diverse and comprehensive realities surrounding spiritual gifts and calling to ministry, because they are designed to help the Church operate at her optimum in the last days. We were created to worship and serve. In other words, man and woman were predestined to be sacred beings, while at the same time fellowshipping with one another.

However, challenges and distortions of the truth, come in various forms to rob us of our divine destiny. No one owns the truth no matter how impressive and elaborate religions and tradition might be. The truth can and must be discovered without prejudice.

Therefore, it must be clearly understood that gifts and callings are freely disbursed throughout the faith community, in order to bring the best out of us. Yes, it is natural for us to admire and compliment talented and gifted individuals who serve in ministry. But under no circumstances should we be intimidated or become mesmerized by the way God uses them.

There is an African Proverb which says, "If a little tree grows in the shadow of a big tree it will die small."

You have the potential to contribute and help make a difference both within and without the faith community; but you must recognize and obey the inner voice. Afterward, it is imperative for you to become disciplined in order to oppose all the negative elements surrounding you. In order to help you grasp the seriousness of these gifts and callings, I have shown you selected Biblical characters cooperating and rebelling against their spiritual mandate.

Please remember that your gifts and callings are tailored made to edify the Body of Christ and simultaneously bring glory to Christ. Your cooperation will make a world of difference just like your rebellion will contribute to the problem. "The only thing necessary for evil to triumph is for good men to do nothing."

I am confident that you will see this publication as an enabling tool for laity and leadership. Gifts and callings have no boundaries. God seems to have a great sense of humor because He is always selecting individuals and distributing gifts and callings to individuals that we would least expect. Case in point is yours truly. I was content being a good person with a variety of ideas floating in my head, or simply wandering through life and bothering no one. However, God called me into ministry and gave me the gift of love for humanity and a special love for the disinherited.

Your life will remain insignificant and void until you stop making others bigger than life, while at the same time boxing yourself in with all sorts of limitations and excuses. You cannot afford to idolize others and belittle yourself. Instead, you must discover the gift and calling within you so that your life will make sense in a senseless world. Gifts and callings fall under the unique heading that I call, *on-the-job training*. Your gift may be a singer, musician, encourager, youth worker, elderly caretaker, fundraiser, administrator, dreamer, visionary, prayer intercessor, armor-bearer and soul-winner etc.

Your calling may be an apostle, prophet, evangelist, pastor, and teacher etc. Whatever your gift and calling may be, I encourage you to be faithful and diligent because your gift will certainly make a difference in the quality of life for all of those whom God has placed along your path.

The Internet can be a valuable tool for communicating wholesome messages. Case in point, one of my friends sent these insightful thoughts to me in 2007. I do not know who crafted this but I know it will be a blessing to you and challenge you to put forth your best at all times. Please do not procrastinate.

There are three things in life that, once gone, never come back:
➤ Time
➤ Words
➤ Opportunity

Three things in life that can destroy a person:
➤ Anger
➤ Pride
➤ Un-forgiveness

Three things in life that you should never lose:
➤ Hope
➤ Peace
➤ Honesty

Three things in life that is most valuable:
➤ Love
➤ Family and Friends
➤ Kindness

Three things in life that is never certain:
- ➢ Fortune
- ➢ Success
- ➢ Dreams

Three things that make a person:
- ➢ Commitment
- ➢ Sincerity
- ➢ Hard Work

Three things that is truly constant:
- ➢ *Father*
- ➢ *Son*
- ➢ *Holy Spirit*

Index

N

Nabi, Hebrew meaning prophet, 23
Naomi, 20, 53
Nineveh, 61
Noah, 11, 19, 45, 46

O

Obama, Barack, 95, 96
Obedience, 19, 41, 46, 68, 74, 76, 85
On-the-job training, 19, 102
Operation Return, 84
ordain, 21, 48, 88, 89, 91, 99
ordination, 88, 89

P

Paraclete, Greek meaning Holy Spirit as Counselor, 28
Pastoral *gift,* 2, 10, 14, 18, 34, 35, 70, 82, 88, 102
patience, 2, 3, 13, 46, 80, 83
Paul, 13, 18, 20, 29, 32, 68, 69, 70, 71, 73, 85, 94, 98
Pentecost, 28, 68
persecution, 74
Peter, 12, 17, 20, 25, 30, 64, 65, 67, 69, 72, 89
Pharaoh, 47, 49
Philippi, 71
Philistines, 55, 57
Phillip, 12, 68
pilgrimage, 84
Potter and the Clay, 60
preacher, 31
  Qoheleth, Hebrew, 31
priest, 22, 23, 54, 59, 60, 62, 76, 89
  call, 25
  kohen, Hebrew meaning, 22
Promised Land, 49

prophet, 10, 11, 18, 23, 34, 35, 39, 49, 51, 52, 54, 58, 59, 60, 61, 63, 72, 76, 88, 90, 102
  nabi, Hebrew meaning, 23
  Prophetic *gift,* 10, 11, 18, 23, 33, 34, 35, 36, 38, 39, 49, 51, 52, 54, 58, 59, 60, 61, 63, 72, 76, 88, 90, 102
Protestantism, 89, 90, 99
proverb, 8, 16, 80, 100
purpose, 3, 8, 16, 18, 21, 22, 24, 26, 31, 44, 74, 75, 83, 86, 97

Q

qadas, Hebrew meaning separated, 79
qahal, Hebrew meaning assembly, 31
qara, Hebrew meaning call, 17
Qoheleth, Hebrew meaning preacher, 31

R

Rahab, 20
rebellion, 5, 7, 33, 44, 45, 51, 55, 61, 64, 69, 71, 72, 74, 97, 101
religious, 20, 33, 64, 75, 88, 90, 91, 93
righteous, 6, 18, 19, 21, 23, 30, 41, 46, 48, 55, 57, 58, 59, 60, 61, 62, 64, 68, 74, 82, 85, 94, 95, 96
Ruth, 12, 52, 53

S

Samaritan Woman, 20
Samson, 20
Samuel, 12, 53, 54, 55, 80
sapel, Hebrew meaning humility, 80

www.ingramcontent.com/pod-product-compliance
Lightning Source LLC
LaVergne TN
LVHW051815080426
835513LV00017B/1968